Poetry

FRENCH TOWN (1928)
DEEP SOUTH (1930)
TAPS IS NOT ENOUGH (1945)
AMERICAN SCRIPTURES (with Carl Van Doren) (1946)

Fiction

GENESEE FEVER (1941)
THE SCREAMING GHOST (1956)

Anthologies

SONGS OF THE RIVERS OF AMERICA (1942)
CAVALCADE OF YOUNG AMERICANS (1958)
THE TAVERN LAMPS ARE BURNING (1964)

Non-Fiction

STARS FELL ON ALABAMA (1934)
LISTEN FOR A LONESOME DRUM (1936)
THE HUDSON (1939)
THE JESSE JAMES OF THE JAVA SEA (1945)
FOR THE RIGHTS OF MEN (1947)
DARK TREES TO THE WIND (1949)
THE YEARS OF GRACE (1958)
THE SUSQUEHANNA (1959)
MY KIND OF COUNTRY (1966)
THE FARM BOY AND THE ANGEL (1970)

Juveniles

THE HURRICANE'S CHILDREN (1937)
AMERICA SINGS (1942)
WILDCAT FURS TO CHINA (1945)
EAGLE IN THE WIND (1948)
HURRICANE LUCK (1949)
TOO MANY CHERRIES (1949)
A FLAG FOR THE FORT (1952)
WINDFALL FIDDLE (1958)
PETS AT THE WHITE HOUSE (1959)
HENRY HUDSON: CAPTAIN OF ICE-BOUND SEAS (1960)
THE HUDSON RIVER (1962)

The Farm Boy
and the Angel

CARL CARMER

The Farm Boy
and the Angel

DOUBLEDAY & COMPANY, INC.
Garden City, New York

1970

Grateful acknowledgment is made to the following:

American Heritage Publishing Co., Inc., for "The Farm
Boy and the Angel," which appeared in *American Her-
itage*, October 1962; "The Death of the Prophet," which
appeared in *American Heritage*, December 1962; and
"Here Is My Home at Last!" which appeared in *American
Heritage*, February 1963. Copyright © 1962, 1963 by
American Heritage Publishing Co., Inc.

CBS Records for material from "The Birth of the Mor-
mon Church" from Columbia Records Legacy Collection
album, "The Mormon Pioneers" (LS1024), Copyright ©
Columbia Records, 1965.
The New York Times for "Peculiar People Prosper" from
The New York Times Magazine, © 1962 by The New
York Times Company. Reprinted by permission.

Acknowledgments

The number of people who have during long years given generously of their time and their abilities to aid the author in his effort to create this narrative is incalculable. He has here listed some of his friends who have been most helpful, and he begs the forbearance of others whose names have unintentionally been omitted.

The late Ralph Beebe
Mr. Hamer Reiser
Dr. and Mrs. David Reiser
Mr. and Mrs. David Evans
Mr. Hugh Brown
Mr. Robert Day
and hundreds of friendly Mormons of the states of New
    York and Utah.
Mr. and Mrs. Sam Weller
Mr. and Mrs. Jay Elson Brandt
Mr. George Shiveley
Mr. Alex Liepa
Mr. and Mrs. Richard Gardner
Mrs. Charles Pearce
Mr. and Mrs. Stephen Danielski
Mr. and Mrs. Orlando Scoppettone

TO ELIZABETH

Foreword

I was born and raised in the region which is now regarded by members of the Church of Jesus Christ of Latter-day Saints (the true name of the denomination popularly known as Mormon) as its "Holy Land." I have written in other of my books of the unique and mystic quality of that part of western New York State. It is a land of narrow blue lakes, of strange pyramidal hills which geology accounts for as caused by the movements of glaciers, of clear-water springs that ignite at the touch of fire, of fountains that leap into sunlight from dark depths of the earth. No region might more excite a boy's contemplative wonder.

At the age of fourteen I once lay, as Joseph Smith reported that he once did, on my back in a leafy grove where the ground was dappled with alternate sun and shade, and listening to voices riding the tremulous air, felt a sense of supernatural presences about me. Hence I cannot find within me a reason categorically to deny that the man whom more than two millions of his fellows regard as a true prophet received revelations which he said had been offered him from a divine source. The histories of all religions abound in narratives of a like nature, all perhaps produced by similar causes within the person or persons to whom they were realities.

Wherever possible, I have chosen not to enter the field of controversy over the truth or falsehood of events which have been said to transcend human experience. Since to do otherwise would completely destroy the purpose of this volume, I have decided to present these chronicles, mostly without comment, as Mormons themselves present them.

Contents

CONTENTS

[14]

The Farm Boy
and the Angel

CHAPTER I

Dark Journey

Just after midnight had ended the twenty-first day of September in the year 1827, tall, twenty-one-year-old Joseph Smith entered the room where his mother lay and asked her if she had a chest with a lock and key. Years later, Lucy Smith told as a memory what happened after she heard the question. She "knew in an instant what he wanted it for, and not having one, was greatly alarmed." Aware of her consternation, Joseph comforted her, saying, "Never mind. I can do very well for the present without it —be calm—all is right."

The young man left his mother on her couch and strode out into the cool of the cloud-blanketed night. A moment later, Emma, his tall, straight wife, "passed through the room with her bonnet and riding dress." To the mother's ears then came the familiar sounds of hitching up, and she realized at once that her son had borrowed the horse and wagon of Joseph Knight, who had arrived on a mysterious business trip from Broome County the day before, bringing with him her son's employer, farmer Josiah Stowel.

When the clopping of hoofs died out, Lucy Smith began an anxious vigil filled with "prayer and supplication to

God." Sleepless in the small frame farmhouse so filled with slumbering folk that it seemed itself to be breathing, she awaited the slow coming of light. In the rooms about her lay her husband, Joseph Sr.; seven of her children, and the two guests. Twenty-seven-year-old Hyrum was her eldest now, since Alvin's death three years ago, when he was twenty-six. Sophronia, "old maid" at twenty-four, had at last found her man and would be married in December. Then came Samuel Harrison—nineteen, William —sixteen, Catherine—fifteen, Don Carlos—eleven, and little Lucy—six.

"At the usual hour," Lucy remembered, "I commenced preparing breakfast. My heart fluttered at every footstep, as I now expected Joseph and Emma momentarily, and feared lest Joseph might meet with another disappointment."

Lucy Smith knew, as her son and his wife began their dark journey, that it was four years ago to the very night when Joseph had first seen the angel. His supernatural experience, as he had told her, had begun even earlier, when he was fourteen. Then, he had been so troubled by the bitter quarreling of proselyting evangelists in the neighboring, hill-shadowed western New York town of Palmyra, that he had walked alone into a grove behind his father's farmhouse and knelt in a sun-dappled, sequestered place to ask God what denomination he should join. Then a pillar of light, sweeping across the treetops, came to rest before the praying boy. In it he saw two glorious beings. One of these spoke, saying that the other was His Beloved Son, and that Other told him to join no sect, but prepare himself for a work to which he was destined. After that, both vanished.

This event had prepared Joseph in some measure for the angel's visit to him in his little bedroom under the eaves. In his report of this, he wrote that in 1823 on the evening of the twenty-first of September as he lay in his bed praying, a light grew about him until his room was brighter than a sunny noonday. Then "a personage" appeared at his side, "standing in the air, for his feet did not touch the floor." He wore a loose robe "of most exquisite whiteness," and his hands and wrists, feet and ankles, head and neck, were bare. Since the robe was open, Joseph could see that he wore no other clothing—"his whole person was glorious beyond description and his countenance truly like lightning. . . .

"He called me by name and said unto me . . . that his name was Moroni; that God had work for me to do; and that my name should be had for good and evil among all nations, kindreds and tongues. . . .

"He said there was a book deposited, written upon gold plates, giving an account of the former inhabitants of this continent and the source from which they sprang. He also said that the fullness of the everlasting Gospel was contained in it, as delivered by the Saviour to the ancient inhabitants; also that there were two stones in silver bows —and these stones, fastened to a breastplate, constituted what is called the Urim and Thummim—deposited with the plates; and the possession and use of these stones were what constituted 'Seers' in ancient or former times; and that God had prepared them for the purpose of translating the book."

Moroni delivered his message three times that night.

On his second appearing, the angel added that the plates and the seer-stone spectacles must not be shown except to those persons to whom the Lord commanded they be revealed. "While he was conversing," wrote Joseph, ". . . the vision was opened to my mind that I could see the place where the plates were deposited, and that so clearly and distinctly that I knew the place again when I visited it." On his third visit, Moroni warned the boy that he "must have no object in getting the plates but to glorify God."

Each time, as the angel messenger departed, the light of the room slowly gathered about him leaving all else there in darkness. And each time, Joseph said, he saw, "as it were, a conduit open right up into heaven, and he ascended until he had entirely disappeared." Immediately after this had happened for the third time, the Smith rooster crowed and the boy, weakened by his tremendous experience, realized that it had taken up the entire night and he must get up at once and begin the labor of a new day.

Working with his father that morning Joseph found himself so exhausted that he could not go on. The older man observed "something wrong" and told his son to go back to the house. As he tried to climb the fence at the edge of the field, he fell helpless to the ground and again the familiar figure of Moroni, standing above him, bade him go to his father and tell of his vision and of the commandments he had received. When he could rise again Joseph obeyed the angel, and Joseph Smith, Sr., having heard his report, told him that the orders of the messenger must be carried out. This matter, said the father, was of God.

Despite fatigue of mind and body, Joseph plodded up

the slope of the nearby hill on which the angel had revealed that the golden plates and the magic spectacles lay. As he neared the summit he was amazed that he recognized every detail of the place from his clairvoyant vision of the night before.

"Convenient to the village of Manchester, Ontario County, New York, stands a hill of considerable size, and the most elevated of any in the neighborhood. On the west side of this hill, not far from the top, under a stone of considerable size, lay the plates, deposited in a stone box. This stone was thick and rounding in the middle on the upper side, and thinner towards the edges, so that the middle part of it was visible above the ground, but the edge all round was covered with earth.

"Having removed the earth, I obtained a lever, which I got fixed under the edge of the stone, and with a little exertion raised it up. I looked in, and there indeed I did behold the plates, the Urim and Thummim, and the breastplate, as stated by the messenger. The box in which they lay was formed by laying stones together in some kind of cement. In the bottom of the box were laid two stones crossways of the box, and on these stones lay the plates and the other things with them."

Eagerly Joseph worked the top rock aside and bent over to lift the discovered treasures. And immediately Moroni, "the messenger sent from the presence of God," was with him for the fifth time, saying sternly that the moment for removing these things was not yet, "but he told me I should come to that place precisely one year from that time and that he would there meet with me, and that I should continue to do so until the time should come for obtaining the plates."

[21]

On the evening of that day Joseph sat up late, informing his family of the new revelations told by the angel. He was so weary, however, that at the suggestion of his brother, Alvin, all agreed to rise early the next morning and to finish the next day's work an hour before sunset. Early supper would then allow a long evening for hearing Joseph's report. And so, when sunset came again, the boy continued his story, first warning his family that what he told them must be held secret. The world, he said, was so wicked that they would be persecuted, perhaps murdered, if they told these things to their neighbors. From that time on the parents continued getting the children together after supper to hear the instructions which Joseph said he was receiving from the Lord. His mother wrote of these evenings years later: "I presume our family presented an aspect as singular as any that ever lived upon the face of the earth—all seated in a circle, father, mother, sons and daughters, and giving the most profound attention to a boy, eighteen years of age, who had never read the Bible through in his life, he seemed much less inclined to the perusal of books than any of the rest of our children, but far more given to meditation and deep study."

CHAPTER II

The Golden Book

It was this same boy, grown to manhood and recently married to brown-eyed Emma Hale, who, with his bride on the wagon seat beside him, drove Joseph Knight's horse to the foot of the familiar hill on the anniversary night of September 21, 1827. There is no record of his meetings with the angel of the hill in the intervening years, save his statements that they took place and that on each occasion he received additional instructions. Nor is there any account other than hearsay of what happened at this reunion when the angel was to fulfill his promise. Believers think it logical to assume that Joseph left Emma in the wagon at the foot of the slope and took his accustomed path to the west side of the summit. There, according to his tell, Moroni awaited him. Since later companions beheld the holy light that surrounded supernatural beings appearing before them, Emma might have claimed to have seen the glow high on the hill where her husband spoke with the tall angel. If she did so, she did not describe it.

Moroni, Joseph wrote later, directed him to take the contents of the stone box but charged him that he should be responsible for them and should not carelessly let them go on pain of his being "cut off." The angel said that he would call for these treasures when he wished them returned, and he bade Joseph to preserve and protect them with all his abilities until that time should come.

Although Joseph's mother could not provide a chest for the golden plates, he may have found one or obtained a substitute that would hide them from human sight. Six years later, one Fayette Lapham, a neighbor, is reported to have claimed that Joseph's father said that his son carried the plates down the hill in a chest which was concealed in a pillow slip. If, as one of the ablest Mormon historians, B. H. Roberts, deduces, neither Emma nor Lucy Smith was aware that morning after Joseph returned home of his actual possession of the golden record, he must have hidden it before returning to the wagon. Fayette Lapham said that, according to Father Smith, a host of devils, yelling hideously, met Joseph as he climbed a fence on his downward journey and one of them struck him so hard that "a black and blue spot remained for three or four days." Joseph did not ever mention these devils. He said only that he hid the plates in a hollow birch log lying in the woods two or three miles from his home. The walk from the bottom of the hill to this place and back must have been long and it is not surprising that Lucy Smith did not hear the sounds of the horse and wagon until after she had served breakfast. Her account of her efforts to conceal the fact that one of her sons had borrowed Mr. Knight's horse and spring wagon and had gone to keep an annual appointment with an angel, offers a bit of rural comedy.

"When the male portion of the family were seated at the breakfast table Mr. Smith inquired for Joseph, for he was not aware that he had left home. I requested my husband not to call him, for I would like to have him take breakfast with his wife that morning.

"'No, no,' said my husband, 'I must have Joseph sit down here and eat with me.'

"'Well, now, Mr. Smith,' continued I, 'do let him eat with his wife this morning; he almost always takes breakfast with you.'

"His father finally consented and ate without him, and no further inquiries were made concerning his absence, but in a few minutes Mr. Knight came in quite distressed.

"'Why, Mr. Smith,' exclaimed he, 'my horse is gone, and I can't find him on the premises, and I wish to start for home in half an hour.'

"'Never mind the horse,' said I. 'Mr. Knight does not know all the nooks and corners in the pastures; I will call William; he will bring the horse immediately.'

"This satisfied him for the time being; but he soon made another discovery. His wagon also was gone. He then considered a rogue had stolen them both.

"'Mr. Knight,' said I, 'do be quiet; I would be ashamed to have you go about waiting upon yourself—just go out and talk with Mr. Smith until William comes; and if you really must go home, your horse shall be brought, and you shall be waited upon like a gentleman.'"

While Joseph Knight talked to his host and sixteen-year-old William Smith searched vainly for the errant horse, the trembling mother heard the reassuring sound of the returning wagon. At sight of her son she was so unnerved that, fearing his mission had been unsuccessful, she left the room. Joseph understood and followed her.

"Do not be uneasy, Mother," he said kindly, "all is right—see here, I have got a key."

Apparently his mind had raced beyond Lucy's to the problem of translating the plates, while she still worried over whether or not he had obtained them. He held out to his mother then the gleaming spectacles Urim and Thummim, the "key" by which he would be enabled to translate the golden record he had hidden in the hollow birch. Lucy took them in her hand and saw them as "two smooth, three-cornered diamonds set in glass and the glasses set in silver bows." With them was a breastplate which her son had wrapped in a muslin handkerchief. "It was concave on one side and convex on the other," she wrote, "and extended from the neck downwards as far as the center of the stomach of a man of extraordinary size."

This article she might well have expected to behold from reading her Bible. A breastplate is coupled with Urim and Thummim in two of the seven books of the Old Testament in which they are named. They seem to have been designated as aids in obtaining understandable guidance from the Lord when He has been formally petitioned. Exodus records the detailed instructions given to Moses by the Lord for the making of Aaron's "breastplate of judgment," which has to be "of gold, of silver, of blue and of purple, and of scarlet, and of fine twined linen," and was to contain four rows of three stones each, arranged as follows: sardius, topaz, and carbuncle; emerald, sapphire, and diamond; ligure, agate, and amethyst; beryl, onyx, and jasper. "And thou shalt put in the breastplate of judgment," said the Lord, "the Urim and the Thummim; and they shall be upon Aaron's heart when he goeth in before the Lord." Moses, according to Leviticus, obeyed implicitly—"And he put the breastplate upon him: also he put in the breastplate the Urim and the Thummim."

After Joseph had concealed the magic spectacles within the house he announced the miraculous news of his discovery to all present. Needless to say, Joseph Knight forgave the borrowing of his horse and wagon, and neither he nor Josiah Stowel left for their homes as they had planned.

The finding of the golden book did not remain a secret. Lucy Smith told a close friend in strict confidence and the news traveled about the whole community with amazing speed. Jealousy rather than incredulity was the immediate reaction. Neighbor Willard Chase, a Methodist "class leader," was so overwhelmed with envy that he at once sent for a noted clairvoyant living some sixty miles away. So urgent was the message that the psychic rode all of a night and a day to arrive in time for a conference at the Chase home, where he swore, "We will have them plates in spite of Joe Smith or all the devils in hell."

In the meantime Joseph had accepted a job. In the afternoon after his return to his home with the diamond spectacles a man named Warner brought him a message from the widow Wells in nearby Macedon. She wished Joseph to come at once to mend her well. Since, as his mother reported, "there was not a shilling in the house" at the time, this was a welcome assignment, and her son had set out at once.

By the next morning, the excitement in the county about Palmyra was so great that the Smith family feared that immediate action would be taken to find and seize the hidden treasure. Emma volunteered to ride to Macedon to warn her husband, and young William was again sent to the pasture to bring in a horse. Soon the girl was on her way, urging her mount to his topmost speed.

Joseph, sensing the possibility of trouble, had come out of the well and he saw her ride up. When he had received the ominous news he went to his employer and told her that important business at home demanded his presence there. Mrs. Wells at first demurred but the young couple were obviously so troubled and so sincere in their request that she ordered a boy to get a horse for Joseph to ride. After a hurried saddling, the excited pair galloped down the Palmyra road and the villagers were soon treated to the sight of their most talked-about neighbors riding swiftly through the streets.

At the Smith house they found Joseph Smith, Sr., pacing nervously back and forth, and Joseph said,

"Father, there is no danger—all is perfectly safe—there is no cause for alarm."

He sent his youngest brother, Don Carlos, to tell brother Hyrum to come at once. Hyrum arrived and Joseph told him to get a chest with a lock and key—and have it ready by the time he returned with the golden plates. Then he set out to retrieve them from their hiding place.

It was about a three-mile walk to the hollow birch but fear of its discovery made the journey swift. The plates were still where Joseph had deposited them, and he began the return walk with the shining treasure wrapped in his farmer's frock. Knowing that he might be attacked if he took the open road, he cut through a heavily wooded section but soon realized that his movements had not gone unnoticed. As he jumped over a large branch that had fallen in a windstorm, someone rose from behind it and hit him with the barrel of a gun. Although hampered by his burden and caught off balance, Joseph turned and struck his assailant to the ground. Sure that the man had confederates nearby, he broke into a desperate run. He had covered about a half mile and was winded and wearied when another leapt upon him from ambush. Again Joseph downed his attacker and ran on. He had almost reached the fence that bordered his father's land when he had to fight off still another vicious conspirator. Terrified and exhausted, he fell over the top rail of the fence and lay still. When he had regained some of his strength, he staggered into the house and told his story. At once his father and the guests, Stowel and Knight, set out to capture the men who had tried to rob him. In a little while they came back empty-handed. At this moment a friend of the family, a Mr. Braman of the town of Livonia, arrived and offered his aid.

Since all were agreed that the countryside had been excited to the point of violence by the story of Joseph's good fortune, the whole group set to work in frenzied haste to raise the hearthstone in order that the golden book, the breastplate and the diamond spectacles might be secreted beneath it. They had hardly completed the job when an armed and angry mob appeared before the house. Here Joseph adopted a stratagem he had learned from the tales of his mother's father, Solomon Mack, who had fought in the American Revolution. Opening all the doors of the little house, he began giving orders in an authoritative loud voice—as if he had many men to command. Then at his signal all of the besieged, even little Don Carlos, ran out as if to attack. The mob wavered—then fled in disorder.

Realizing that their enemies would soon return in greater force, the Smiths and their friends considered how best to outwit them. They raised the hearthstone once more

THE FARM BOY AND THE ANGEL

and took from under it the box that held the treasures. Joseph lifted them out, covered them with cloths, and carried them to a cooper's shop across the way. Here he climbed into the loft where lay a pile of flax and hid his precious burden beneath it. Then he nailed the cover back on the box, tore up the floor of the shop, set the empty receptacle below, and replaced the floorboards.

When darkness came the mob returned. This time there was no stopping them. They swarmed about the Smith house searching every inch of ground but finding nothing. By this time they had lost faith in the imported conjurer and were placing their confidence in Willard Chase's sister who, having found a stone of a strange green color, claimed that by looking into it she could see "where Joe Smith kept his Bible hid." Apparently, her assumed clairvoyance had led to the box, for in the morning the Smiths found the floor of the cooper shop once more torn up and the wooden chest splintered into many pieces. The treasures were safe in the loft beneath the flax.

This is the "origin story" of the religious sect known formally as the Church of Jesus Christ of Latter-day Saints; informally, as "the Mormons." All conversion to the Mormon creed begins with the acceptance of this miracle-fraught narrative. John Henry Evans, Mormon historian, who has written one of the most objective and thoughtful biographies of Joseph Smith, delivers plainly the accepted Mormon attitude: "Mormonism has its basis on the miraculous element in religion, or it has no foundation at all on which to stand. They are fooling themselves, whether within or without the Mormon Church, who think they can accept the faith of Joseph Smith and at the same time reject the visions of Joseph Smith. No such choice is permissible. One must believe these supernormal experiences and Mormonism, or one must reject Mormonism with the visions."

CHAPTER III

Flight from Vermont

When young Joseph Smith was ten years old his mother bore another son—romantically christened Don Carlos. The new baby was the ninth of her children and only one, Ephraim, had died. The prospect of having to feed ten mouths moved the father to set out from his high barrens above the Connecticut River at Norwich, Vermont, and seek an opportunity for a better living in newly developed lands to the west. With him went a like-minded neighbor named Howard. Considerations other than unfertile soil strengthened the decision of these men, for this was 1816, ever afterward reviled as "old eighteen-hundred-and-froze-to-death." Because most of their crops froze, the Yankees called it "poverty year" or, since the only food obtainable was from the coast fisheries, "mackerel year."

From a high perch above the White River, the older Smith children and their mother with her baby could see irregular blotches on a cold sun. In early June came almost intolerable heat and, suddenly, sunspots again and snow and fierce cold that froze the new-plowed acres hard. After that, each day dawned to bright frost and dry weather. Even cold-weather birds—goldfinches and scarlet sparrows—took refuge in houses, where people could pick them up in their hands to warm their numbed bodies.

In July snow lay on the summits of the Green Mountains. The smoke of wood fires dimmed the wintry weeks of a summer that had vanished. For a hundred and twenty days there was no rain. A farmer said that when he was mowing the lower forty on the Fourth of July, he had seen an antlered buck leap a stone fence and land in a snowdrift so deep that he could not extricate himself before the swinging scythe had decapitated him and provided fresh venison for a large family.

In the midst of this long drought, unexpected hope came to the Smiths. Mr. Howard appeared at their door to tell Lucy that in western "York State" he and her husband had come upon the busy town of Palmyra in which they thought they might prosper. Father Smith had sent word to the family to sell what they could not pack, pay their debts, and accompany Mr. Howard when he set out on his return.

No sooner had she told her Norwich neighbors that the family was moving west than they gathered like vultures. Knowing that the decision was final, they made ridiculously low offers for the farm possessions and she was forced to accept them. Soon Mr. Howard was clucking to the Smith team, and the overloaded Smith buckboard was rattling south along the valley road.

Lucy was forty years old that summer. With her new baby at her breast and eight older children, she was leaving the mountains she had always known and making the journey to the Genesee country, far across the state of New York.

The mother soon discovered that Mr. Howard, the one

adult male of the expedition, was dissatisfied and suddenly uncooperative. He disciplined her children strictly and she quarreled with him over his treatment of young Joseph. He had decided that the older children should walk as much of the way as possible. Samuel Harrison, eight; William, five; Catherine, four; and baby Carlos were obviously too small to keep up with the wagon. Joseph was still recovering from an operation that had taken place two years before. A primitive surgeon without aid of anesthetic had lanced an infection of his knee and, cutting deep below it, had scraped the bone. The boy had been sent afterward to his uncle, Jesse Smith, who lived at Salem, Massachusetts, in the hope that salt sea air might improve his general condition, but he still limped. Howard ignored this and ordered him out of the wagon time and again.

When the Smith caravan left the old Dutch town of Albany on the Great Western Turnpike, they were not alone. Hundreds of Yankee farmers, disheartened by the stony soil and freezing weather, had pulled up stakes and were rolling west to the fertile ground and the mild climate which they had been told they would find beside the fresh-water seas. Promise of thriving business lay in every swaying stagecoach that plunged past, in every freight wagon thundering over the deep-rutted road with the driver cracking his long whip over the eight-horse team. Peddlers' wagons—"flying stores"—jingled to a stop here and there and the owners exhibited glittering wares and shouted their praises. Taverns along the way swarmed with loud-voiced patrons and hurrying servants.

At one of these hostelries, about twenty miles west of Utica, Lucy Smith, preparing in early morning for another day on the road, heard the excited report of her son Alvin that Mr. Howard had thrown their goods on the ground and was about to drive off with the wagon and team. She told the boy to order the driver to the barroom. He came and they met in a noisy crowd of travelers. Lucy demanded an explanation and Howard answered that the money she had given him for the trip had run out and he had quit.

The blood of her Scottish preacher ancestors, the spirit of her soldier father, Solomon Mack, who had fought the French and Indians, and later the British, asserted themselves. She spoke out so loudly and so sharply that the chattering men and women about her were stilled. The whole scene made such an impression upon her memory, she wrote years later, that she could recall her every word. "Gentlemen and ladies," she said, "please give your attention for a moment. Now, as sure as there is a God in heaven, that team, as well as the goods, belong to my husband, and this man intends to take them from me . . . leaving me with eight children, without the means of proceeding on my journey."

She turned to Howard. "Sir," she said, "I now forbid your touching the team or driving it one step farther. You can go about your own business; I have no use for you. I shall take charge of the team myself; and hereafter attend to my own affairs."

Then she walked out to the horses and took up the reins while Howard, fearing the temper of the crowd, slunk away.

The lame, grave towhead would walk little now. He would ride and think, and he had more to think on than most boys on the west-rolling wagons. In his first decade, and possibly before his memory took hold, his parents had moved him from their Sharon farm, boulder-peppered, steep and lonesome above the tumbling White River, to busy Tunbridge.

In that town before his birth, his father had once set up a shop and his mother had tended it, and the two of them had risked their savings on a profitless venture—shipping ginseng roots to China where this commodity was said to be in great demand as a reviver of sexual potency.

They found the return to Tunbridge with little Joseph disappointing and set out for nearby Royalton which also had failed them once, and now did so again. Then they tried Lebanon, New Hampshire, in Connecticut's smiling valley. By this time Joseph was about seven and fully aware of his changing environs. For several months here the family did so well that they could afford to enter Hyrum at Moore's Academy a few miles north at Hanover. From this school he came home with a fever instantly communicated to his brothers and sisters. Thence came the infection on Joseph's leg and the savage operation. Once more the family moved back to Vermont and a fertile Norwich farm which kept none of its promises because of three crop failures in successive years, the last being in desolate 1816.

During all the peregrinations through little Yankee towns, Joseph had known two old men who had left their marks upon him. One was white-haired Grandfather Mack who, come a-visiting, would painfully climb down from the sidesaddle on his rib-striped mare to tell the family stories of the days when he was a hero in battles against the painted, whooping Indians, the slick and monstrous-cruel monseers, the dim-witted British lobster-backs. When Joseph was five the old man had brought the Smiths a book in which his tales had been printed, and daughter Lucy never tired of reading them to her children.

The other old man was Grandfather Azael Smith, tall and well filled out but of strange appearance because a burn on his neck when he was young caused him to carry his head to one side—"Crooked-neck Smith," folks called him. He, too, had fought in the War of Independence and so had his father—but he said little about it. He was a thoughtful man who had ideas and stuck to them even when the whole of Topsfield, his home town in Massachusetts, disagreed. He was a man to talk about a boy's behavior and his work and his thoughts about God. He was both serious and powerful but of a gentle nature never seeking trouble though he never avoided it either when it came his way. Joseph had not seen as much of Azael Smith as he had of Solomon Mack, but Azael was not someone to forget.

Most recent of Joseph's memories and most vivid as he bounced along on the buckboard was the seaport, Salem, which he had left only a few months before his father had set out for the West. To a Vermont farm boy whose parents were almost continually on the move, this town could not have failed to provide a symbol of continuing wealth, stability, and romance.

The big many-windowed houses enhanced by neat trim and neater fences, looked as if they had stood for generations as indeed some of them had. The lovely doors that opened on Essex Street, Washington Square and Chestnut Street offered entrance to rooms filled with elegances that had come from far—mahoganies from the West Indies, silvers from England, porcelains from China. The families who owned them, richly dressed and dignified, walked the cobbled streets as if they knew of no other world of sterile acres and mounting debts. Down by the harbor docks, where merchant wanderers of the sea rocked at anchor and the winds freed wild odors of Canton tea, Brazilian coffee, and spices from a hundred islands, dark-visaged sailors spat and swore and embroidered narratives of their adventures. Among the Salem boys who looked and smelled and listened, there was one, dark and handsome and a year older than Joseph, Nathaniel Hawthorne. This boy's father, a sea captain, had died in Surinam when his son was four. Since, at the time of Joseph's visit, Nathaniel was very lame from an injury in a ball game, the boys may have found a bond in their common affliction. Nathaniel was one day to reveal in his books the influence of his Salem surroundings upon him. That they had a lasting and significant effect on sensitive, blond Joseph as well is not to be doubted, though few of his biographers have suggested it. The town had caught his fancy, and years later he would come back to Salem still believing that priceless treasures brought from across the ocean had been concealed in some of its old houses.

And so, for a ten-year-old, Joseph was something of a sophisticate as he journeyed toward Palmyra. He had had several homes in small Vermont towns, he had known disease and had withstood almost intolerable pain, he had visited in a seaport where talk was of the world rather than of a county, he had experienced many an inexplicable and wondrous act of nature (attributed in his time only to the wishes of God). As later associates, both enemies

and friends, discovered, he had a kind of blotter mind
that soaked up at once such facts and impressions as interested him.

There was much along the Great Western Turnpike
that would fascinate a boy of this sort. After his mother
had rid herself of Howard and taken command, the Smith
party passed through busy Manlius where four turnpikes
spreading like rays from a star, crossed each other. Beyond it lay Green Pond (unblinking eye of shadowed
water set two hundred feet below the precipitous bluffs
that were its shores), and nearby a well digger had come
upon an echoing cavern so spread beneath its grotesquely
shaped ceilings that no man could say how far it extended
or what might be found within it.

These sights proved to be omens, forerunners to the
Smiths of stranger phenomena that they would find when
they neared their journey's end. The long slopes of the
York State hills began to flatten out as they approached
Palmyra. The Great Western Turnpike led them neither
up nor down and the horses trotted easily on a spreading
plain striped by narrow blue lakes and dotted with green
pyramids. They had entered the land of the drumlins.

Few settlers thought of these greenery-covered piles
of earth and rock as created in the ice age by glacial
action. Their neat geometric design and their smallness
suggested that they were man-made mounds, cones of
earth erected by prehistoric tribes, and that they might
contain precious relics of a long-forgotten era.

There is no detailed description of the arrival of the
Smith family at Palmyra and their reunion with father
Joseph. Since they were a loyal and affectionate group
it can be assumed that, though Lucy had only two

pennies and a small portion of their belongings left, it was joyous. It signalized, moreover, a period of intense activity for them all. Twice as big as Norwich, Palmyra was a bustling town of over three thousand and it anticipated a rapid and limitless expansion. On the expected route of the Great Western Canal which Governor De Witt Clinton was determined to build, the town saw itself within a few years a widespread commercial port on a man-made river. Father Smith could well expect that the "cake and beer" shop which Lucy at once started would do well. Gingerbread, boiled eggs, pies, and root beer found eager customers, particularly among the children of the town, and Lucy added to them for trade with adults oilcloth table covers which she had a knack for decorating with colorful designs.

CHAPTER IV

A Place to Wander In

The drumlin country and its environs held wonders that
fascinated its inhabitants who had come, for the most
part, from New England, a land of less startling natural
phenomena. They felt now as if they had entered a ring
of enchantment. At Bristol, south of Palmyra, springs
brushed by a torch bubbled into blue and yellow flames.
A few miles from these strange waters every detail of the
variegated world of woods and rocks had become part
of one wide monochrome—yellowed by spattering dye
from the sulphurous fountains of Clifton. Where their
acres had not been cleared, the settlers gaped at towering exotics—tulip and cucumber trees—or at a hollow
buttonwood in which a church elder had preached to a
congregation of thirty-five. (He said reprovingly that it
would have held fifteen more.) Plowmen uncovered, lying
like a log in the earth, many a bulbous root—three or
four feet long and six to eight inches in diameter—which
looked for all the world like a nude male body. "Man-in-
the-ground" they called it and they speculated darkly on
its powers. Colored stones of fantastic shapes jeweled the
banks of meandering Mud Creek, and now and again among
them flashed a prism of translucent selenite which old-

sters called moonstone because, they said, it waxed and waned with phases of the moon. This was a land for a boy to wander in. It stirred a sensitive mind to creative imaginings.

As strange as the atmosphere created by the drumlin country was the talk of the people. Only a few of the pioneers were learned, and superstition stirred the others into unchanneled reckonings. There were long-continued discussions of the ignorant farm girl Rachel Baker, a neighbor who had amazed the countryside for the past two years by preaching eloquently in her sleep. Hundreds came from miles around to her home at Scipio on Owasco Lake to see her rise from her bed, though still slumbering, and hear her incredibly scholarly sermons often embellished with "poetical quotations." Soon it was necessary to provide her a couch in a public hall where more pilgrims could profit by her sleep-born homilies. Said one of her hearers who came on a night of wind and rain:

"The deep attention of the auditors, the sighs of the women, the pattern of the hall, the howling of the tempest, united with the speaking corpse, as it appeared uttering its awful warnings of mortality, offered one of the moments of retirement to the soul, when we shudder and shiver in sublimity."

The miracle had influenced Father David Rathbone to transport the remarkable girl in his carriage all the way to New York City to be examined by America's most famous authority in such matters, Dr. Samuel Latham Mitchill. That gentleman, a member of the Columbia University faculty, at once wrote a book about Rachel's case and in it presented examples of other uneducated persons who had been subject to what he called "Devo-

tional Somnium" and empowered by God to speak learnedly while asleep. By this time the folk of the eastern
states had been so moved by Rachel's story that they
took up a collection for her education. In 1816, as young
Joseph Smith was entering the region she had just left,
she had been entered in a private and refined school for
girls on Hudson Street in Manhattan, much to the disapproval of many of her former neighbors, who felt that
the work of God should not thus be tampered with.

The boy would come much closer to another and more
powerful personality in the next few years. She, too,
seemed by background and schooling completely un-
equipped for the work which, she assured all who would
listen, had been chosen for her by God. It was her claim
that in 1776, when she was Jemima Wilkinson, an un-
schooled maiden of eighteen, she had expired of a fever
in Rhode Island. No sooner, she said, had her soul left
her slim, lithe body than the "Spirit of Life from God"
had inhabited it. At once she had risen from the dead pro-
claiming herself the "Publick Universal Friend." Though
she could not read, she proved herself divinely inspired
by her knowledge of the Bible, all of which she could
quote from memory, and her speech was so laden with
God's truth, so her followers said, that she won the devotion of hundreds. Because she was darkly beautiful and
emotionally persuasive, more than two hundred of these
migrated with her to the country of the Finger Lakes
shortly after 1790. There, in her purple robe and white
beaver hat—low-crowned and broad-brimmed—she ruled
her people as a queen who derived her authority from the
Almighty.

Her palace was a large white house on the shores of

Crooked Lake (now Keuka Lake), and there seven pretty handmaidens sought to fulfill her every wish. At her right sat lovely and youthful Rachel Malin—heir apparent to her kingdom—and at her left, in the white robes of a prophet, James Parker, "the spirit of Elijah," who was accustomed on occasions he thought propitious to draw his girdle so tight that his belly swelled out above it like a balloon, then to announce that he was filled with the wind of prophecy and deliver occult utterances with an assurance frequently accepted by "The Friend" and her people as proceeding from direct communication with the Lord.

In 1816 Jemima Wilkinson was fifty-eight and her striking beauty had vanished. She would die for the second time ("leave time," she called it) in three years, but she was still the autocratic leader of her people. Young Joe Smith heard much of her upon his arrival in the drumlin country and, since she was still very active in attending to what she considered the needs of her flock, he may have seen her, pitifully fat and dropsical, behind the fluttering damask curtains of her coach, which shone like an uptilted half-moon above wheels that glittered through the dust of the turnpike.

It is unlikely that the spindling yellow-haired lad, tall for his years, dreamed in those days of ever becoming the third of the region's religious "originals" whose lack of formal education rendered their achievements in the eyes of those who believed in them inexplicable save through the miraculous power of God. Nevertheless, a few years later when he was bitterly assailed as an ignorant though cunning charlatan, he may have taken some comfort from the fact that hundreds of good and honest people had believed in the divine origin of the words that came from the mouths of Rachel Baker and the Publick Universal Friend.

For the two years that followed their exodus from Vermont, the Smith family earned and saved in and around lively Palmyra. There were wells to be dug, farms to be cleared, harvests to be reaped; and father Joseph and his sons were employable. When such work was scarce they diversified the articles for sale at their shop by making split-wood baskets, kegs, churns, wooden flails for threshing. By 1818 they had enough money to make a down payment on a hundred acres of wild land two miles south of Palmyra and near the largest of the drumlins. Here they raised a substantial log house, and when a thaw signaled the approach of spring they tapped so many of their sugar maples, it is recorded, that they manufactured from one season's flow of sap three and a half tons of maple sugar, a record that made them proud winners of a bounty of fifty dollars as the leading producers in Wayne County.

Joseph was now tall enough and strong enough to do a man's job. How he happened to be in the woods that edged the Susquehanna River at Great Bend, Pennsylvania, is not known, but the writings of a companion who lived in that area at the time, one J. B. Buck, recall an important event that colored the rest of his life. "Joe Smith was here lumbering soon after my marriage which was in 1818, some years before he took to 'peeping' and before diggings were commenced under his direction. These were ideas he gained later."

Mr. Buck said that Jack Belcher (the Belchers came

from Union Hill in Gibson Township) had shown Joseph a stone that he said would give to those who looked upon it in darkness clairvoyant powers. Jack had bought this "seeing-stone," as he called it, when he was working with the saltmakers at Salina, in York State. Mr. Buck wrote that he had often seen the Belcher stone himself. "It was a green stone with brown, irregular spots on it. It was a little longer than a goose's egg, and about the same thickness."

Such a talisman was not a new concept among Pennsylvania and New York settlers at this time. James Fenimore Cooper in his novel *The Pioneers*, which depicted Cooperstown as it was in 1793, wrote that one of his characters (Jotham) "acknowledged before he died that his reasons for believing in a mine were extracted from the lips of a sybil who, by looking in a magic glass, was enabled to discover the hidden treasures of the earth." The author then added the explanatory note, "Such superstition was frequent in the new settlements." These sentences were written in 1823, a year when Joseph was especially active in "glass-looking" (popular phrase for the use of seeing-stones), and would seem to indicate that when Joseph beheld Belcher's purchase, such aids to psychic vision had been in popular use in America for at least a generation. There is the possibility at least that report of Joseph's "money-digging" on the Susquehanna just south of the New York border at the very time Cooper was writing his book at the river's source had brought clairvoyance to the writer's attention.

Belcher let it be known that his green-and-brown treasure was for sale. He added, as proof of its value, that when he had brought it back to his Pennsylvania home and covered it with his hat, his little boy, who had been first to peep into the darkness under the brim, had seen it glowing like a lighted candle. Upon looking a second time, said the father, his son exclaimed, "I've found my hatchet," and ran to the spot where that article had been lying lost for two years. After that the boy had been asked by many neighbors to look into the stone and tell them where to find things they had misplaced, and he had "succeeded marvellously," having even been able to trace the wanderings of a lost child who, when found, was dead from starvation.

That this prize would excite in a boy of Joseph's temperament a desire for possessing it was inevitable. He bought the stone, wrote Mr. Buck, though he did not say how much of the young lumberman's hard-earned and scanty wages was exchanged for it. Joseph at once tested it and reported that he saw treasures in the earth near Red Rock—where the likeness of a giant chief, painted by a prehistoric Indian artist, decorated a perpendicular stone surface beside the Susquehanna.

Disappointment in the project was attributed not to the inefficacy of the stone but to the diggers' failure to maintain strict silence while at work—one of the primary rules of the then current orally transmitted manual of treasure-digging. Mr. Buck said Joseph claimed that, because of this error, "the enchantment removed the deposits."

If Mr. Buck's reminiscences are trustworthy, Joseph seems to have bought his first seeing-stone only a short time before he beheld, according to his own testimony, the vision which first revealed his appointment to his divine mission. He had hardly returned from the Susquehanna's wooded banks when a wild religious revival, a sort of spiritual forest fire, swept into Palmyra from the eastern coastal states where it had been raging for months. Ardent, ambitious Jesse Townsend, recent graduate of Yale, began it with the intensity and fervor of youth, and success brought to his side a fellow Presbyterian, Preacher Stockton from East Palmyra. At once, and at the invitation of these evangelists, the Baptist minister joined in and so did Methodist Preacher Lane. Soon, however, what had seemed an inspired alliance of the three denominations in the cause of protestant Christianity, turned into strife between them.

Fourteen-year-old Joseph found himself in an agonizing quandary. His mother Lucy, his brothers Hyrum and Samuel Harrison and his sister Sophronia were all, as he was to write in 1838, "proselyted to the Presbyterian faith." Nevertheless, he had been moved by the strenuous appeals of the Methodist spellbinders.

The bitter animosity which each of the sects directed toward the others gave the boy no peace.

"In the midst of this war of words and tumult of opinions, I often said to myself, 'What is to be done?'" A chance reading of the Epistle of James, first chapter, fifth verse, gave him the answer: "If any of you lack wisdom, let him ask of God, that giveth to all men liberally, and upbraideth not; and it shall be given him."

Joseph said it was on a clear and sunny morning of early May in the year 1820 when he decided to take this advice. He had found a secret, quiet place and like many another boy of his age he took pride in feeling that by right of discovery it was his own. A quarter of a mile behind his home he climbed a gentle slope edged with young beeches and a tangle of shrubbery, to a summit where stood a company of tall sugar maples. An opening among the leaf-hung branches allowed a shaft of yellow sunlight to penetrate the shade. There was a stillness here, overwrought with almost inaudible sounds—bird calls, the hum of bees, the whisper of foliage as the air drifted in a movement too gentle to be called a breeze. Here was a refuge from the pressures exerted by the shouting preachers, the emotional hymns, the outcries of hysterical penitents. Here as he lay on his back in the shade of the high maples, he believed peace might enter his tortured mind. Not peace, he reported later, but darkness enveloped him—". . . it seemed to me for a time as if I were doomed to sudden destruction . . . and at the very moment when I was ready to sink into despair . . . just at this moment of great alarm, I saw a pillar of light exactly over my head."

Consciousness of the material world left him, he said, without his being aware of its going; for all seemed real as before except for movement among the tiny particles that danced within the gleaming column, a massive changing into distinguishable forms of light existing within light. He saw, or dreamed he saw, two figures suspended there, heard, or dreamed he heard, their voices.

"I asked the personages who stood above me in the light, which of all the sects was right. . . . I was answered . . . that all their creeds were an abomination."

When the luminous gods had uttered their message and vanished from the bright shaft, Joseph said, he came to himself again, lying on his back and looking up into heaven. His mind had been freed of its torment.

The vision and the voices, despite their intimations that he was chosen to fulfill a divine purpose, had not, however, created a sense of consecration to a mission promised but unexplained. After he had told one of the Methodist evangelists of his experience and been ridiculed for his pains, he put aside the idea of conversion to any denomination. Being a sociable, growing adolescent, he gave himself over to such enjoyments as came naturally to a youth of his time and in his region. Even the first visit of the tall angel, Moroni, when he was seventeen, did not deter him from worldly pleasures. In his late twenties, after the birth of Mormonism, Joseph frankly admitted this fact: "As is common to most, or all youths, I fell into many vices and follies . . . and those imperfections to which I allude, and for which I have often had occasion to lament, were a light, and too often, vain mind exhibiting a foolish and trifling conversation."

Most available descriptions of Joseph Smith as a boy were written after he had become the founder of the Mormon Church. They show resentment that such a youth became important enough to command public attention; shock at his claims, which were regarded as sacrilegious; suspicion that he was a charlatan and to be regarded with amused contempt. Any testimony in his favor could be regarded then as unwilling and therefore worth considering. A learned historian, O. Turner, who recalled Joseph's walking in to Palmyra village from the Smith farm two miles out on Stafford Street, remembered that the boy once a week strolled into the office of the old *Palmyra Register* for his father's paper and sometimes did odd jobs at Scovell's store. "I can see him now in my mind's eye," reported Daniel Hendrix who had been a typesetter in those days, "with his torn and patched trousers held to his form by a pair of suspenders made out of sheeting, with his calico shirt as dirty and black as the earth, and his un-combed hair sticking through the holes in his old battered hat."

This lake-country prototype of Huckleberry Finn combined in his person strangely fascinating qualities. Said Hendrix, "Joe had a jovial, easy, don't-care way about him that made him a lot of warm friends." Pomeroy Tucker, one of the owners of the *Palmyra Sentinel*, remembered that the boy was proverbially good-natured—yet he was never known to laugh. All witnesses agreed that he was both imaginative and articulate. According to Tucker, Joe caught a spark of Methodism in the camp meeting away down in the woods on the Vienna road and became a very passable exhorter "in the juvenile debating club that used to meet in the red schoolhouse on Durfee Street," and, to quote from Hendrix again, "He was a good talker and would have made a fine stump-speaker if he had had the training. He was known among the young men I was associated with as a romancer of the first water. I never knew so ignorant a man as Joe to have such a fertile imagination. He could never tell a common occurrence in his daily life without embellishing the story with his imagination; yet I remember he was grieved one day when old Parson Reed told Joe he was going to hell for his lying habits."

From these descriptions emerges a personality not at all inconsistent with the New England whence Joseph Smith came nor the area in which he grew to manhood. The narrator who told exaggerative tales with a straight face was a widely admired figure of the time. The title "biggest liar in the county" was highly prized and eagerly sought by every narrator of popular oral fiction. Joseph's grandfather, Solomon Mack, was just such a storyteller. The superstitions of his neighbors had given Joseph's impressionable and eager mind fascinating materials, and from them he had fashioned a world of miracle and wonder. Hence, he could well be grieved when Parson Reed confused his creative literary imaginings with immoral lying. A modern psychiatrist, aware of manic-depressive cycles, might add an interesting note to modern concepts of the boy upon reading a contemporary's testimony that "at times he was melancholy and sedate, as often hilarious and mirthful," though the sentence can hardly be accepted as justifying any conclusion.

Since the great majority of his community identified all semblances of the supernatural as the works of either the devil or the Lord, it was inevitable that he should do the same. A contemporary said that Joseph told him his power to use his peep stone as an instrument of clairvoyance came from God. If he believed this, his occult practices after his first vision, which were harshly criticized, would seem consistent. Since he was more sensitive, fanciful and articulate than those who inhabited the small, suspicion-ridden world in which he lived, it is not surprising that he won spreading fame for supernatural gifts. Among those who later turned against him with bitter words were men whose greed for buried gold had led them to believe that he possessed occult powers and to employ his services as a clairvoyant.

Whatever his motivations, Joseph was still susceptible to the wonder of small stones. In 1822, he and others were digging a well for the Chase family in nearby Manchester, when, at a depth of more than twenty feet, appeared an opaque stone "of a whitish glassy appearance" and shaped "like a child's foot."

This gleaming grotesque so captured his speculative mind that he bought it at once and enlisted its magic. When it was in his hat and his face was down over it to exclude all light from outside, said neighbor Joseph Capron, he could see by its radiance objects of great wonder—"ghosts, infernal spirits, mountains of gold and silver." Either this stone made different impressions on those who saw it or his lapidary collection had grown to three before he announced his discovery of the book of golden pages, for the stone, which he later said held the same translational powers as the diamond lenses of the spectacles he found beside the book, was described by two who said they saw it as almost black—one witness adding "with light-colored stripes."

Apparently, the discovery and purchase of the "child's foot" stone added to Joseph's reputation. Although he was but seventeen, he was equipped with the recognized implements of a glass-looker and his was the name that came immediately to mind throughout the region whenever there was talk of buried treasure and the spells exerted over it by concealers long dead. According to later testimony of his neighbors, he had acquired much of his comprehensive knowledge of occult lore from a peripatetic magician, conjurer and fortuneteller named Walters, who had no sooner wandered into the nearby town of Sodus than he had been jailed for the crime of "juggling." Undiscouraged by the coldness of his welcome, Walters let it be known that for three dollars a day he would make use of his supernatural gifts, his divining rods (peach, witch hazel, and mineral), his crystal spheres, and his stuffed toads, in finding Indian gold and chests of Spanish coins lying beneath the surface of many an otherwise unproductive farm. A disapproving local journal, the *Palmyra Reflector*, reported that Walters once "assembled his nightly band of money-diggers in the town of Manchester, at a point designated in his magical book, and drawing a circle around laborers with the point of an old sword and using sundry other incantations," sacrificed a rooster to propitiate the spirit of the place, but all his ritual proved to no avail.

When Walters had resumed his vagabondage, the *Reflector* ironically and jocosely suggested that the mantle of the town's former mystic had fallen upon young Joseph Smith. When in 1833 Joseph, founder of the Church of Jesus Christ of Latter-day Saints, excommunicated from that body in Kirtland, Ohio, handsome Philaster Hurlburt for "unchristian conduct" toward the females of the sect, Philaster raced to Palmyra to beg from more than a hundred of the prophet's former neighbors affidavits exposing his sinful conduct in the years before he claimed the discovery of the golden plates.

While the statements obtained are highly suspect (since most of them do not repeat information given by others and since all are couched in Hurlburt's style), they furnish an authoritative manual of the wildly poetic folk-concepts with which Joseph's brain boiled during his adolescence. Many who testified against their erstwhile companion (Willard Chase among them) had firmly believed in the superstitions they now jealously cited as proofs of the wickedness and deceit of the boy whose mind had absorbed them. According to the affidavits, Joseph had at various times offered the following suggestions to treasure-diggers:

The best time for digging money is the summer, when the sun's heat draws ancient coffers "near the top of the ground."

A chest of gold watches lay in the earth of Joe Capron's farm, but it was retrievable only if a man brandishing a burnished sword marched on the surface above it to protect the diggers from assaults by the devil himself.

In a hill on the Cuyler farm was a cave "containing an immense value of gold and silver, stands of arms, also, a saddle for a camel hanging on a peg at one side of the cave" since "the ancient inhabitants of this country used camels instead of horses." There were other caves, too, and one sheltered "barrels and hogsheads of coined silver and gold—bars of gold, golden images, brass kettles filled with gold and silver—gold candlesticks, swords," all in charge of spirits clad in ancient dress.

To find such riches, hire a glass-looker, blindfold him and bid him kneel. Then hold before him at eye level a tall white hat in which his seer-stone lies concealed and he will see the place you seek.

To possess the treasure take a black sheep to the spot, cut its throat, and lead it bleeding in a circle that the red drippings may penetrate the earth and appease the ghastly guards below.

Or, dressed in black and riding a black horse with a switch tail, gallop to the place and demand the treasure in a certain name. As the chest rises from the earth, lift the lid and take your prize, but beware the blinking toad beside it that in a trice becomes a man and knocks you three or four rods with one blow.

Avoid, too, uncovering the dark stone with a white spot the size of a sixpence in its center. It lies in shallow soil nearby and when light makes it visible, it swells to the size of a twenty-four-pound shot and explodes in shattering thunder, causing your treasure to vanish utterly.

CHAPTER V

The Magic Year

New impulses swept western New York as the year 1825 began. Not since the coming of the Yankees, exiled by 1816's cold summer, had the countryside been so stirred. Already commercial craft were plying long sections of Governor De Witt Clinton's man-made river, which was to be completed and opened in the fall, and profits were said to exceed the golden dreams of their owners. The Erie Canal towns of Wayne County, home of the Smith family, were boiling with expectations.

From the east to nearby Sodus on the shore of Lake Ontario came a colony of Shakers, and immediately the nervous religious ferment of the past decade intensified. The Shakers' insistence on asceticism, celibacy, cleanliness, and quiet contrasted strangely with their worshipful rituals. Visitors reported that their religious exercises included dancing and whirling and marching, which moved them to such ecstasies that participants broke from the rhythmic pattern and, receiving "the gift of tongues," howled out long passages of unintelligible gibberish.

From the east, too, came the Irish laborers on the canal, and their presence in the miasmic Montezuma swamps had added the melancholy of their native music and the humor of their tall tales to local folklore. The ghostly voices of malaria-slain diggers called at night above the bogs between Geneva and Seneca Falls, and the stings of mosquitoes, blown up by Celtic fancy to the size of well drills, pierced the iron sides of sap kettles.

Spring was slipping into summer when out of the west on the placid waters of the new channel floated a gala craft, bearing the old Marquis de Lafayette. The boy hero of the American Revolution, now sixty-eight, had returned in the previous year to the land he had fought for, and his triumphal tour of it was soon to end. He had given the lake-country towns short notice of his visit, but they were ready for him. At Rochester a flotilla of twelve flower-strewn, pennant-hung barges awaited his arrival. Brass bands on their decks crashed into "Hail, Columbia" and "Hail to the Chief" and an artillery company let go air-shattering salutes as his boat slipped under bridges laden with cheering, waving admirers. The canal's banks were thronged, the city's rooftops covered, its windows packed, as the populace raised "shouts of joyful acclamation." Said a newspaper—the *Rochester Telegraph*—a week later, "They were going to him, by the thousands, on the spot which he had known only as an unexplored wilderness. They were going to receive him on that channel which is so proud a monument of 'publick enterprise and publick patriotism.'"

The cannoneers of Canandaigua, gathered hastily at their guns, welcomed the tall, wizened general that evening with salvos heard far across Canandaigua Lake, and the town's spacious hotel produced a feast for a hundred distinguished guests. By ten o'clock next morning a lake-to-lake journey had been made and the nation's most welcome visitor, in an elegant barouche drawn by six milk-white horses, rolled into Geneva heralded by massed bands and the "roar of ordnance" echoing over Seneca's waters. In the public square, Lafayette marched under a hastily constructed arch and "along a carpeted way strewn with flowers" to a new-built stage. After the speech-making, then, and the tearful meetings with comrades of battles long ago, the young ladies who had strewn the flowers sang an ode "especially composed for the occasion." When Lafayette re-embarked on the canal that evening at Syracuse, having covered seventy-five miles by coach in twenty-four hours, the towns through which he had passed were already contentedly regarding the day's efforts as only a rehearsal for the autumn celebration soon to come when the waters of Lake Erie would at last be linked with those of the Atlantic and the harvests of the boundless West might be dispatched on waterways to the markets of the world.

On October 26, the *Seneca Chief*, new canal packet, made her way from Lake Erie into the completed "Hellespont of the West," hailed by thousands of the citizens of Buffalo. The *Young Lion of the West*, bearing in cages on her decks two wolves, a fawn, a fox, four raccoons and two eagles, awaited her in Rochester. As the water parade made majestic progress through the drumlin country, farmers and townsfolk raced across the fertile fields, described only a few years before as "so barren 'twould make an owl weep to fly over them," to become witnesses of a new wonder of the world. Workers who had labored during the day were guided to the procession by fireworks bursting in the night sky. Golden reflections emanated from the water, for an unending aisle of barrels, like dark stubby candles, spurted flames above the channel, and the air was thick with the pungent, almost choking, smell of burning tar. Distant gunfire produced a steady thudding which was interrupted now and then by the reverberating crash of a nearby cannon. Figures appeared on the boat decks waving toward the shores and excited spectators tried to identify the Governor of the State of New York, De Witt Clinton, the distinguished, long-haired scientist, Samuel Latham Mitchill, the mayors, judges, professors, of neighboring towns.

While there is no specific proof that nineteen-year-old Joseph Smith, money-digger and farm hand, saw either of 1825's wildly applauded spectacles, there can be no doubt that they had an influence on him, as they did on everyone else in Western New York. Since he was the grandson of two veterans of the Revolution, and Canandaigua was a scant nine miles from his home, there is a strong possibility that he made the opportunity to see the noble Frenchman and his cortege somewhere along the route. And being of the nature he was, it is unlikely that Joseph missed the ceremonies attendant upon the consummation of the "marriage of the waters" which had been awaited by all the area for eight long years. Perhaps indeed his love of parades and uniforms and pageantry, patent in the days when he himself received the huzzas of a worshipful populace, stemmed from those moments of that magic long summer when the visions of the shining barouche and the prancing white steeds, the light-filled canal and the elegant packets flashed upon his eyes, when his ears were enchanted by the brassy chorusing of the bands and the thunderous booming of the guns.

In mid-autumn of 1825, farmer Josiah Stowel of South

Bainbridge, a Chenango County town on the Susquehanna just north of the Pennsylvania border, had traveled over the long Western New York State hills to Palmyra. He had a double purpose in mind—to visit relatives and to talk with the glass-looker, Joseph Smith, who, he had heard, might be able to divine the place on his acres where Spaniards had long ago mined silver. He offered Joseph fourteen dollars a month "and found" to go to his farm with him, and, in a few days the boy, his father, and Stowel were on their way. At the end of their journey the Smiths were "put to board" at the home of a prosperous hunter, Isaac Hale, who lived in the Pennsylvania town named Harmony.

Mr. Hale and his wife's brother, Nathaniel Lewis, had brought their families by oxcart from Vermont to the banks of the Susquehanna in 1787. The journey had been dangerous but, as a local historian who knew them remarked, "They had heard Ethan Allen swear and so were not afraid of bears."

The Hale household was a big one the fall that Joseph Smith was a part of it. The father, then sixty-three, had sired five sons and three daughters. Thirty-eight years of hunting on the New York State frontier had developed him into a familiar American type—the experienced and wise old woodsman—much the same character as the fictional "Leatherstocking," whom novelist James Fenimore Cooper was creating out of materials furnished by the lives of Daniel Boone and others like him who lived nearer to his Cooperstown home. Isaac Hale and his boys must have used all their woodcraft and hunted early and late in Ichabod Swamp, on Turkey Hill, and along the Starucca and Pigpen Creeks to fetch enough meat for the family and treasure-hunters. Nine years afterward Isaac recorded that the Smiths (father and son) "and several other money-diggers boarded at my house . . . digging for a mine that they supposed had been opened and worked by the Spaniards many years since." At first the hunter had believed in the project but he later said that Joseph had disillusioned and disgusted him by announcing that his peep stone was failing him because of a more powerful counter-enchantment.

Among the women serving the hungry men in those weeks of night digging, a slim, tall, dark daughter of the house caught Joseph's eye. By nature twenty-two-year-old Emma Hale was taciturn and reserved and she was soon sitting, wide-eyed and silent, beside Joseph while he unburdened his mind of the wonders that teemed within it.

When the expedition, despairing, shouldered spades and departed in mid-November, its glass-looker went back to Josiah Stowel's farm, but he returned again and again throughout the snowy winter to woo the hunter's daughter. Meanwhile, he worked for Stowel, went to school, and kept on peering into his dark talisman to behold in its glow, if he could, the riches his employer confidently expected him to find. Whenever the weather allowed, Josiah sent word to his diggers to assemble and Joseph led them after darkness had fallen across the river flats to scramble up the steeps of the surrounding hills. Countless old coins, the diggers dreamed, lay buried on Bend Mountain, heavy gold on Monument Hill, and under a slope near the South Bainbridge farm, salt-laden waters burbled.

Torches flared on the ridges above the valley towns while the diggers recited incantations to break the spells laid upon the ground into which they sank their spades. Then, as spring began, one Peter Bridgeman, intolerant of such goings on, swore out a warrant for the arrest of Joseph Smith as "a disorderly person and an imposter."

Joseph was brought before a Justice of the Peace at Bainbridge on March 20, 1826. Of the five witnesses at his trial, three told of their certainty that the defendant could "divine things" by "looking into a hat at his dark-colored stone." One of these said that Joseph had told him how a money trunk was situated and that after he had dug down several feet for it he struck upon something sounding like a board or plank. At this moment, the witness testified, Joseph remembered that the last time he looked into his stone he had seen the two Indians who had buried the trunk quarreling until one slew the other and threw his body into the hole beside the trunk where it remained as a spirit-guard. It had proved its protective power, the witness continued, for as the digging went on, the trunk kept sinking and remained constantly at about the same distance from the diggers.

Despite the testimony of the three who believed in Joseph's mystic powers, however, two scoffers appearing for the prosecution found more favor with the judge. The trial record states, ". . . the Court finds the defendant guilty."

No report of the sentence has been found. If there was one, it must have been either light or suspended, for Joseph continued his work on the Stowel farm throughout the rest of the year. Isaac Hale, on being asked by

Joseph for his consent to marrying Emma, replied with a stormy No. No stranger, he said, and certainly not a glass-looker, could marry a daughter of his. And so throughout the summer of 1826 Joseph, whenever he could leave the Stowel farm, made journeys southward that ended in clandestine lovers' meetings. To the good fortune of the couple, scarceness of game in the increasingly settled Susquehanna Valley took the hunter far afield and often kept him away from home for several days.

CHAPTER VI

Morgan

It was in the Indian Summer days of Joseph's courtship of Emma Hale that there befell a third event, which would have an even greater aftereffect on him than the pomp and show of the two pageants that had stirred the countryside. Whether the young lover was at his father's home during the second week of September, 1826, or surreptitiously meeting his sweetheart by Susquehanna's winding stream is not known, nor is it very important, for the story of what happened in Western New York during those few days was to shock the whole nation and influence the thoughts not only of Joseph Smith but of thousands of other Americans for years to come.

William Morgan, a hotheaded Virginian who had served as an officer under General Andrew Jackson at the Battle of New Orleans, had settled with his wife and children at Batavia, official seat of Genesee County. Morgan claimed to be a high-ranking member of the Ancient Order of Masons and persuaded neighboring fellow members to apply to a chapter of Royal Arch Masons in nearby Le Roy for permission to establish a similar lodge in Batavia. Somehow, perhaps because he was a hard-drinking, boastful man, the applicants suspected that Morgan was not of as high position in the fraternity as he claimed, and would not allow him to sign their petition. The insult enraged him, and, in his Virginian's code, cried for revenge. A friend of his, Colonel David Miller, was also a veteran of the recent war and a dissident Mason. Miller was owner of the town newspaper, and the two ex-soldiers made no secret of the fact that they planned to print an exposé of the secret rites and purposes of Masonry. Morgan would write it, Miller would publish it, and fellow citizens who were not members of the Order would buy it to discover how dangerous were the Masons' ambitions to circumvent justice where fellow members had broken the law, or to control the nation's affairs by electing Masons to high office.

In the middle of the night of Friday, September 8, forty masked men in fantastic dress marched in quick catlike steps in the dust of a Batavia street and halted before Miller's print shop. At once flames leaped within it, and the vandals took up again their muffled tread. A tramp who had chosen to sleep nearby in an empty stage-coach broke the silence then with loud cries. Lamps flickered on in the windows of Batavia and doors slammed as men raced from their homes. Their attack on the blaze succeeded. The presses were saved and could still print Morgan's book.

The Masons, who had decided to take into their own hands the carrying out of such horrific penalties as violation of their fraternal pledges, met secretly to plan other ways of thwarting their enemy. On Sunday morning a Canandaigua magistrate issued a warrant for Morgan's arrest on charges of stealing a shirt. A constable and a posse of five reached Batavia that night. In the morning, they arrested Morgan, beating down Colonel Miller's frantic efforts to protect him, and began their return journey with their prisoner. The next day Morgan pled that he had only borrowed the shirt and was released but his persecutors quickly charged him with failure to pay a tavern bill of $2.69 when last in Canandaigua, and he was remanded to jail.

On the heavy, hot night of Tuesday, September 12, repeated knocking brought the jailer's wife to her door, where suave men told her they had come to pay Morgan's debt and procure his release. The woman said her husband was absent, and that releases late at night were not customary, but the men finally persuaded her to let the prisoner go. As Morgan walked down the jail steps, there was a sudden scuffle, then a man's voice crying, "Help! Murder!" to the quiet, moonlit town. A yellow, curtained carriage drawn by a team of fast-trotting grays flashed into the empty street and drew up to the curb. For a moment men struggled in its black shadow. Then there were no more cries—only the sound of horses' hoofs beating the powderlike, crumbling earth of the road's surface. By morning the yellow wheels had rolled as far as Hanfords Tavern, just outside of Rochester. There waited a team of bays hitched to another carriage, black and funereal. All that sun-seared day the abductors and their victim were borne west along the Ridge Road. A solitary outrider kept a mile ahead, and in three towns fresh teams were quickly substituted for horses sweat-whitened by the heat. At Newfane, close to Lockport, the lights of Wrights Tavern peppered the dusk. Inside at long tables the management was serving a dinner for men only. Between courses guests strolled to the drive-barn where, grotesquely slumped on the rear seat of the carriage, lay a bound, gagged, masked figure.

At ten o'clock the journey continued. It reached its end at the small, round powder-chamber of old Fort Niagara where the captors locked up their charge. Few doubt now that soon thereafter they murdered him and threw his body into the Niagara River.

To a lovesick young man these events, at the time of their happening, may have meant little. The stormy disapproval of his sweetheart's father may have seemed more important to him personally, or a rendezvous during old Isaac's absence from home on a hunting trip may have drawn him away from the stage-set of the melodrama. Nevertheless, the crime and the shocked talk it aroused were to make a lasting impression on Joseph Smith.

By the end of the year the lovers could wait no longer. They sought the aid of Josiah Stowel and it was eagerly given. On January 18 of the new year of 1827, Joseph met Emma secretly for the last time and drove her to South Bainbridge. There in the home of Squire Tarbill they were married by Tarbill himself. Almost immediately, and probably to escape the wrath of the bride's father, they set out for Manchester where they received a hearty and approving welcome. The neighbors were too excited at this time by the murder trial in Canandaigua of the men who had attacked and transported William Morgan, to give much attention to a runaway bride, and Joseph, now facing responsibility as a husband and potential father, happily set about the farm duties allotted to him by his father and his brothers. These, to a young man whose life had already proved his intolerance of boredom, must have seemed dull indeed, but he was buoyed up by a

consciousness that before long something would happen—
an event so momentous that it would change the course
of his life in miraculous ways. Whether, as over two
million good Mormons believe today, he was waiting in
awe and reverence the return of the angel who had
promised him that in September he would at last receive
the book of golden pages lying in the nearby hill, or
whether, as skeptics have suspected, he was planning the
perpetration of the most amazing hoax in history, the
spring and summer of 1827 must have been a time of
almost breathless anticipation for the tall and thoughtful
bridegroom as he went about his homely and overfamiliar
tasks. Seedtime came and went; the heat of summer danced
above the hills and waters; the September harvest was at
hand.

At last came the moonless dark of the night of the
twenty-first. Outside their home in the nearby Cayuga
County town of Aurelius, a twenty-six-year-old carpenter,
painter and joiner, Brigham Young, and his young wife,
Miriam, stared long at the western sky. Years afterward
this man, whose name would be linked throughout
posterity with that of Joseph Smith, remembered that
they had seen a strange light there, which was "perfectly
clear and remained for several hours." As they continued
to look, ". . . it formed into men as if there were great
armies in the West; and I then saw in the North West
armies of men come up. They would march to the South
West and then go out of sight. It was a very remarkable
occurrence. It passed on, and continued perhaps about
two hours." At about that moment Joseph Smith had
prepared himself to make what he later said was his fourth
annual ascent of the Hill of Cumorah.

CHAPTER VII

The *Book of Mormon*

The members of the faith of the Church of Jesus Christ of Latter-day Saints are often disturbed by the fact that non-believer historians are inclined to attribute the *Book of Mormon* to Joseph Smith's personal authorship and to regard its content as influenced by the spirit of the times and by topical events. These "Gentiles" (Mormon name for all non-Mormons) do not give credence to Smith's narrative of his communication with the angel Moroni who directed him to the spot on Cumorah Hill where he discovered a book of golden pages. On these, he reported, were inscribed a history of much of South America, and the story of Christ's visit there after his crucifixion. Since the body of the history given in the *Book of Mormon* is so extensive as to prohibit its being meticulously summarized here, perhaps the simplest way to characterize it is to report one of its most important narratives which states that Jesus Christ, after the crucifixion and resurrection, appeared in South America where He again chose twelve disciples. Before His eventual ascension He gave each of the twelve the choice of going with Him on his ascension or of awaiting the judgment day on earth. Three chose the latter and, known as "The Three Nephites,"

still wander this world doing good deeds. Smith's translation of this book, which he said was written in "Reformed
Egyptian" by Mormon, the father of Moroni, was accomplished by the use of wide spectacles of a marvelous
nature that were found with the volume. Its content is
regarded as sacred by all Mormons. They believe it to be
quite as inspired as the Bible, to which it is complementary,
and they look upon it as a further testimony to the truth
both of Christ's experience and his teachings. Such sim-
ilarities as exist between the incidents told in this account
of ancient tribes of the western hemisphere and the events
of Western New York history, Mormons regard as evi-
dences that "history repeats itself"—a truism that no historian, regardless of his religious faith—denies.

Opinions of the *Book of Mormon* when its distribution began in 1830 were mixed and extremely positive.
Many of the translator's neighbors who had never before
doubted that buried treasure might be found through clairvoyance were now so jealous of the twenty-four-year-old
discoverer of the strange book that they denounced him
with almost incredible bitterness. On the other hand, a
number of the readers of the volume believed in it—
partly because it was written in a Biblical style, partly
because they had wearied of the violence and prejudice
of the bickering that had gone on among Presbyterians,
Baptists and Methodists in their disputes over which denomination should obtain increase of membership after the
evangelists had won converts. Young Joseph had witnessed
the conquest of his father, mother, and older brother,
Hyrum, by Protestant sects. He had himself at one time
exhorted in favor of the Methodists. Finally, sensitive and
distraught, he had wandered into a sun-stippled grove and

there knelt to pray for guidance. In answer, he said, he had received a divine revelation that all the teachings of the denominations were "abominations" in the sight of God and he should join none of them.

Though a number of the young prophet's enemies, in their effort to discredit him, contended that he had not the intent of establishing a religious creed and eventually a church when he released the *Book of Mormon*, no intelligent reader of that volume, believer or non-believer, could fail to see that it created a structure of faith. Whether it be a historical record of ancent times written by the angels Mormon and his son Moroni and translated, with the aid of God, by an uneducated country boy, or the creative product of that boy's imaginings, the fact remains that no scholar has yet discovered that the boy had obtained enough schooling to be capable of writing it. Claims that a contemporary was the author have long since vanished into nothingness. Nearly two million Mormons have faith enough in Joseph Smith's chronicle to believe it. The number of Christians who do not is infinitely greater. There is no question that the book had a unique appeal at the time of its publication. It flatly denied the threats of the evangelists. It argued for calm reason rather than stormy emotion. It was optimistic rather than dour. It was non-denominational and as a contemporary preacher, Alexander Campbell of the denomination known as the Disciples of Christ, wrote, it covered "every error and almost every truth discussed in N. York for the last ten years."

Aside from its religious comment, the book also espoused political concepts which the citizens of the new nation found entirely reconcilable with their own patriotic enthusiasms. Converts liked the idea that contemporary Americans might become "latter-day" saints just as Abraham and Isaiah had been "early-day saints" in the times described in the Old Testament. They liked a narrative which gave historic importance to their own region. They were happy because the book told them that men in the days before Christ had had problems similar to their own and had adopted such symbols of revolt against tyranny as Liberty Poles. They argued that, just as the founding fathers of the United States had returned to fundamental truths found in Plato's *Republic* and in the works of English John Locke and other philosophers, so the *Book of Mormon* opened the way to the Restoration of the True Gospel—neither Protestant nor Catholic.

Though great numbers of the population of America regarded the *Book of Mormon* as blasphemous and sacrilegious, there were many men of education and higher-than-average mental excellence who read the volume and became converts.

Others who were well read jeered at the book and ridiculed it for its repetitions of such Biblical wordings as "Behold" or "And it came to pass" (which appears about two thousand times). It has been argued that the Bible had become so familiar to the settlers (most of whom had no other volume) as to cause readers of the new book to overlook such expressions as mere conventions. Mormon and Gentile readers alike have complained that the profuse use in the *Book of Mormon* of "Behold" and "It came to pass" is an all-too-apparent effort to imitate the style of the King James translation of the Christian Gospels. It has been argued by some sympathetic scholars, however, that since the writings of Mormon and Moroni were translated from "Reformed Egyptian," it is possible that the meaning of these expressions may have been delivered by single letters or characters of that language and were intended only to convey the idea of a past tense. Contemporary readers who choose to disregard the too-oft-repeated clauses completely will discover that the remainders of sentences so introduced often fall into simple and direct and sometimes rhythmic prose.

On March 26, 1830, the *Book of Mormon* was put on sale in Palmyra's one bookstore. Eleven days later six young men, all under thirty years of age, met where the rolling acres of the Peter Whitmer farm bordered the fresh waters of Seneca Lake. They were gathered in the very region described by sentences from the *Book of Mormon* which Joseph Smith had dictated to Oliver Cowdery, a Palmyra schoolteacher, a few months before—"And it came to pass that we did march forth to the land of Cumorah and we did pitch our tents about the hill of Cumorah; and it was in a land of many waters, rivers, and fountains . . ." There the six organized the Church of Jesus Christ of Latter-day Saints. On that Tuesday, standing before five of his fellows—Oliver Cowdery, Hyrum Smith, Peter Whitmer, Jr., Samuel H. Smith, and David Whitmer—Joseph Smith reported he had received a revelation from God, which began: "Behold there should be a record kept among you: and in it thou shalt be called a seer, a translator, a prophet, an apostle of Jesus Christ, an elder of the church through the will of God the Father and the grace of your Lord Jesus Christ."

In his autobiographical report of the occasion, Joseph Smith later wrote that he and Oliver Cowdery ordained each other as elders of the new church and "some prophesied whilst we all praised the Lord and rejoiced exceedingly."

The number of converts grew rapidly in the next few months but not as rapidly as the ambitions of the young leaders.

The members of the church filled their arms with copies of the *Book of Mormon* and wandered about the countryside selling them from door to door. An interesting description of Joseph Smith as he appeared in a barn on the "Lake Road" near the town of Geneseo tells that ". . . he had on cowhide shoes and pepper and salt stockings and brown blue trousers—blue overhalls and a batiste shirt and a brown vest and no necktie but a big agate button that rode up and down his Adams apple."

Missionaries were soon to go to the British Isles, to other European countries, even to the faraway islands of the South Seas. They encouraged the belief that if the prophet would submit even his minor problems to the Lord, divine revelations would direct him to their practical solutions. Though persecutions had already begun, they had full confidence that neither Joseph nor his followers would ever lack courage to meet them. There would come a time, said the seer, when the church would settle on western lands near the Lamanite (American Indian) tribes and its troubles would cease.

CHAPTER VIII

Night of Angels

On a late January dawn in 1831, young Newell K. Whitney wakened in his home town—a scattering of comfortable Ohio farmhouses called Kirtland by its owners—and set about the chores of early day. As junior partner of the community's General Store (the sign above the front door read GILBERT AND WHITNEY), he busied himself about the banked fire in the stove and the arrangement of the wares on the shelves. Then he heard the familiar sounds of a two-horse team crossing the Chagrin River bridge a short distance to the north, and the long whoa! of the driver of a wide sleigh which was stopping at the foot of the outside store steps. A tall man had thrown off his covering blanket and was bounding up toward him. The door opened and a cheery voice said loudly, "Newell K. Whitney, thou art the man!"

Recovering from the shock of this surprising hail, the embarrassed storekeeper said, "You have the advantage of me, sir. I cannot call you by name as you have me."

"I am Joseph the Prophet. You have prayed me here—now what do you want of me?"

Behind the tall smiling Prophet, Newell saw the well-known face of Preacher Sidney Rigdon, who eloquently conducted Sunday services in Kirtland's one church or in the Church of the Disciples a few miles up the road, in Mentor. The storekeeper knew that the whole area during the week had been aflame with evangelical meetings. He was in good company and he "cottoned to" the Prophet at once. By noon of that day Joseph was living in the merchant's home and Newell had become his lifelong votary.

A score of New York State Saints straggled into little Kirtland the next day, crowding the town. They had been distributing copies of the *Book of Mormon* among the farm families near Rochester and Lockport and Buffalo. The devout citizens of Geneseo and Avon and Canadaigua and of the already religion-ridden Yankee towns of Connecticut and Massachusetts were pouring long westbound processions of wagons, carts and even oxcarts onto the turnpikes. So many copies of the book had reached the people of New York's western towns that the roads west were suddenly alive with converts to the new religion it taught. The boards of the Little Chagrin River bridge set up a continuous rumbling and it seemed that every bob-sled and carriage, every buggy, every sleigh in the eastern states had taken to the Kirtland road.

Sidney Rigdon, newly baptized into Joseph's faith, thundered from his pulpits, and his hearers were so shaken by what he said that they fell to their knees, then lay prostrate shouting, screaming in the anticipation of a great City of Zion near Ohio's eastern border. But when the youthful Prophet Joseph told them the story of the book of golden plates, or reported how the wide spectacles that lay beside them in the earth had enabled him to translate the Neo-Egyptian narratives which had been engraved upon them, his clear, strong voice and his apparent logic silenced his hearers and had them nodding their heads in approval.

Joseph's imaginings ever throughout his life led him into more ambitious dreams. The snowball of his faith had been set rolling and was enlarging itself with gathering impetus.

Trusted converts were sent west as missionaries to the Indians, and when they arrived, they discovered that many Gentile pioneers (besides brother Mormons) had gathered in Jackson County, Missouri, and were already waiting for the new religious teachings. Kirtland, he realized, could never be Zion. The country beyond it in the vastness of the prairies and the mountains was, in Joseph's mind, the perfect dwelling place for all his people—so beautiful and peaceful that it would eventually become the place of "the gathering."

But Kirtland could and should have a temple. The Lord had told him this in a series of revelations—revelations so explicit that he could draw the plans not only for one temple but a dozen more, and he did so in case they would be needed.

When Joseph had received the first of the temple revelations he reported some of the Lord's sentences as follows:

"Verily I say unto you, that it shall be built fifty-five by sixty-five feet in the width thereof and in the length thereof in the inner court. . . . And there shall be a lower court and a higher court according to the pattern which shall be given to you hereafter."

With the precise aid of the Almighty, the Prophet, now thirty years old, assembled the Mormon workers, who began to raise the three-story building from the summit of a gentle slope into the Ohio clouds. The lower story held two sets of pulpits—one set on the western end, the other on the eastern. Tall curtains to be hung within would divide the enclosed rectangular area into four rooms for small audiences.

Each month saw the walls go higher. The men who climbed the ladders were painters, carpenters, wood carvers, joiners, glaziers, and each of them was determined that the building should be worthy of its title, "The House of the Lord."

Elaborate patterns asserted themselves in and above the carved window frames. Warmly grained woods from Ohio groves appeared in the floors and beams. Strengthening grains turned sturdy corners. Porcelain shards of Yankee treasure mottled the rising walls, while the shiny remains of York-State glass-house tumblers dropped like hail into the drying mortar that would give them permanence. Then the top gables were done. The men who had finished them were not the religionists who had dreamed them into the sky. They were the day-by-day, month-by-month artisans, each giving his prideful skill to the final achievement.

There came a day in the early spring of 1836 when these workers could look above the treetops and see across twelve river-haunted miles the white-spattered Chagrin, where it entered the blue of Lake Erie. With a rush then came the quick-spreading knowledge that the short spire they had finally pointed upward was signaling that the moment of the dedication of the Lord's House was at hand.

Once more the air was filled with the dust of Mormon

wheels. People came early from every direction and awaited patiently the opening of the doors. Out in the meadows of Kirtland on the day of March 2 grazed countless tethered horses, and the wagons they had drawn were lined up in neat long rows. Many of the great company of travelers had arrived in the night, and at seven o'clock the earliest arrivals surged through the entrances of the temple.

Joseph and his associates in the three-fold Presidency, Oliver Cowdery and Sidney Rigdon, acted as ushers and showed to their seats nearly a thousand Mormons. So many were refused entrance that another meeting was scheduled for the schoolhouse. Even this arrangement proved unsatisfactory and hundreds of eager families were turned away. Inside, the most prominent of the Mormon Church officers sat at one end of the long room in two groups, each centered about one of the two pulpits.

Brother Joseph, President, Seer, and Revelator, offered the first prayer, admonishing the audience to establish "a house of learning, a house of glory, a house of order." As he finished, the choir (seated in four corners of the room) began a hymn which ended as Sidney Rigdon began to speak. No sooner had he done so than a high-ranking member of the faith stood up and said that an angel had come in the window and sat next to him throughout Brother Joseph's prayer. Among others who confirmed this statement later were Joseph Smith (who included it in his *History of the Church*) and Brother Heber C. Kimball, who reported in his autobiography that the angel "was a very tall personage, black eyes, white hair, and stoop-shouldered; his garment whole, extending to near his ankles; on his feet he had sandals."

Throughout all of this exciting meeting the Mormons, becoming more and more excited, had been applauding at the end of each section of the program with what was coming to be known as the "Mormon Shout." Apparently, though the words were not always identical, and though it occasionally appeared in printed Mormon songbooks, it was shouted rather than sung. Such "shouts" were not unique in America's social history and one at least has come "down through the family" of this author. The first line was always a question shouted by one man:

"Who was General Washington?"

And then all present would shout in rhythmic cadence,

"First in war

First in peace

First in the hearts of his coun - try-men!"

So it was that the "Mormon Shout" had raised the spirits of an audience of a thousand on that wildly exciting evening of March 27, 1836. Brother Joseph realized that this was the most important assembly of his people since the church had been founded on Lake Seneca's shore. He was exalted to report its successful conclusion:

"A noise was heard like the sound of a rushing mighty wind which filled the Temple, and all the congregation simultaneously arose, being moved upon by an invisible power. Many began to speak in tongues [the language Adam used in the Garden of Eden] and prophesy; others saw glorious visions; and I beheld the Temple was filled with Angels, which fact I declared to the congregations. The people of the neighborhood came running together (hearing an unusual sound within, and seeing a bright light, like a pillar of fire resting upon the Temple) and were astonished at what was taking place. This continued until the meeting closed at eleven P.M."

The week went on with prayers and visions and prophecies, and at the end of the week, Joseph, Sidney Rigdon and Oliver Cowdery once more went into the crowded temple and secluded themselves behind the curtains. When they came out, Joseph said:

"We saw the Lord standing upon the breastwork of the pulpit, before us, and under His feet was a paved work of pure gold in color like amber.

"His eyes were as a flame of fire, the hair of His head was white like the pure snow, His countenance shone above the brightness of the sun, and His voice was as the sound of the rushing of great waters, even the voice of Jehovah."

CHAPTER IX

March to Zion

It was near the Christmas of 1833 when the builders of the Mormon Temple at Kirtland had first become aware of tragedies in the western land their Prophet had chosen to call Zion. In Jackson County, Missouri, and other places nearby, the Gentiles had begun such persecutions of their Mormon neighbors as could not be tolerated. Night raids in the area had left Mormon houses blazing and Mormon people suffering the pains of wild violence. Missouri mobs had tarred and feathered innocent men and were demanding that their victims leave the homes on which they had legally settled, and surrender the lands they had happily claimed months before. Women and children had felt the lash of whips, the brutality of clubs, the fearsome threats of armed ruffians. Jackson County, upon which Brother Joseph had centered his hopes for a possible Zion, was bent on driving the Mormon people out into a wilderness that teemed with hostile Indians and dangerous wild animals.

The governor of the state had made strenuous protests, had spoken again and again in defense of the state laws which the land robbers were violating, but to no avail. Then on Washington's Birthday, two of the Prophet's best friends, Lyman Wight and Parley Pratt, arrived in Kirtland to report as eyewitnesses the outrages committed on the Mormon families of Missouri.

The next day action was swift. Brother Joseph said he was on his way to Zion. He asked for volunteers to go with him and about fifty responded. Elected "Commander-in-Chief of the Armies of Israel," the Prophet made no secret of his intent to restore Zion and to cause, by force if necessary, the return of Mormon lands to their rightful owners. At that moment came a revelation in which the Lord gave His orders for action and comforted them by saying:

"Let no man be afraid to lay down his life for my sake . . . for whoso layeth down his life for my sake, shall find it again. . . ."

Further recruiting began at once. The volunteers looked for weapons and found dirks, knives, pistols, rifles, tomahawks, and, for their commander, a sword said to be four feet long.

On May fifth, every male citizen of Kirtland, aside from Sidney Rigdon, Oliver Cowdery, and elderly workers on the temple, marched proudly out of the town bound for Zion. The whole force by that time consisted of a hundred men. They halted that evening at New Portage and began organizing their unit. The dividing of their undrilled volunteers into tens and twelves with a leader for each proved a pattern that Mormon pioneers would find successful in the years to come.

As the marchers passed through Mansfield, Ohio, the next day, they gave hearty welcome to a band of Vermont Yankee Mormons who joined step with them. A week later they had crossed the Miami River and were happy that they were advancing at a rate of about forty miles a day. In steady rhythm they marched past Indianapolis and they exulted as they crossed the Mississippi. Recalling these days, Brother Joseph later said:

"Angels went before us and the faith of our little band was unwavering. . . . We know that angels were our companions, for we saw them." Every night their trumpet shook the darkness, bidding them sleep. Every morning awakened them to rise and trudge onward.

Now the claim jumpers of Missouri were alarmed. They were determined to protect the lands which they had occupied after forcing the Mormons from them. Missouri, they said, must not be defiled by religious fanatics; they would give their lives to prevent it and they kept up their persecutions of Joseph's little army all through the summer and the early autumn. An eloquent citizen stood in Jackson County Courthouse and hurled defiance at the invading horde:

"The citizens of Jackson are determined to dispute every inch of ground, burn every blade of grass, and suffer their bones to bleach on their hills rather than the Mormons should return to Jackson County."

Scholars who have read this paragraph have noted that it resembles the rhythm and content of the late Sir Winston Churchill's famed challenge to Germany. Some have pointed out that Sir Winston had the opportunity to read it when he was on a lecture tour through the Middle West during the early months of World War II. Perhaps, they say, the Prime Minister happened on it in the back files of the Liberty, Missouri, newspaper called *The Upper Missouri Enquirer* and took inspiration from it for his later challenge to Hitler, which has become a classic.

[85]

Confrontation was inevitable. The marchers, doing their best to simulate an army, even held a mock battle in which one of them grasped an opponent's sword and severely cut his hand. Other difficulties harried them. Two comrades wakened from sleep to find a pair of prairie rattlesnakes curled beneath them. Their drinking water became putrid with tiny red living animals. A thunderstorm of amazing proportions floated their beds, and frightened both the waiting Missourians and the Mormons. The Fishing River rose to unprecedented heights, threatening to drown both opposing forces, and it so frightened the Missourians that they withdrew to their homes.

Joseph said at once that the storm was "of God" who was punishing the wicked men who had stolen lands from the Mormons and driven them from their homes.

On the midnight of October 25, the sleeping newly created Mormon town of Far West, Missouri, wakened to the beat of a brass drum in the village square. A splatter of tuneless trumpet notes sounded above it. A torch appeared and then a crowd. A hoarse voice was reading a bulletin describing crimes committed against the Mormons the day before. The torch revealed a flag—a fluttering white field and in its center the blood-red legend "PEACE." Beside it the half-dozen horses of a mounted guard reared and plunged. A quickly muted cheer came from the crowd as David Patten—"Captain Fearnot," they called him—in a white military jacket, gave quick and low-voiced orders. About sixty men began to march away from Far West toward Crooked River.

"The Missourians are coming," someone said—"the damned Pukes are after us."

The gleam of dawn was on the horizon when the Captain halted his command. Brother Joseph halted with them. No one has written of the following events more simply or directly than he, and the account should be told in his words:

. . . It was just at the dawning of light in the east, when they were marching quietly along the road, and near the top of the hill which descends to the river that the report of a gun was heard, and young Patrick O'Banion reeled out of the ranks and fell mortally wounded. Thus the work of death commenced, when Captain Patten ordered a charge and rushed down the hill on a fast trot, and when within about fifty yards of the camp formed a line. The mob formed a line under the bank of the river, below their tents. It was yet so dark that little could be seen by looking at the west, while the mob looking toward the dawning light, could see Patten and his men, when they fired a broadside, and three or four of the brethren fell. Captain Patten ordered the fire returned, which was instantly obeyed. . . . The fire was repeated by the mob, and returned by Captain Patten's company who gave the watchword "God and Liberty." Captain Patten then ordered a charge. . . . The parties immediately came in contact with their swords, and the mob were soon put to flight, crossing the river at the ford and such places as they could get a chance. In the pursuit, one of the mob fled from behind a tree, wheeled, and shot Captain Patten, who instantly fell, mortally wounded, having received a large ball in his bowels. . . .

Brother Patten was buried this day [October 27] at Far West. . . . I could not help pointing to his lifeless body and testifying "There lies a man that has done just as he said he would—he has laid down his life for his friend."

[87]

The death of Captain Fearnot and a sudden epidemic of cholera so lessened the number of marchers to Zion that they were panic-stricken. Brother Joseph, realizing the failure of the expedition, disbanded his command, some of whom returned to Kirtland. The Missourian authorities took advantage of the weakened enemy to capture the Prophet and several of his comrades. There were many sudden onslaughts then and men on both sides were wounded or slain. The Missourians had become so incensed by the Mormons' strong defense that they killed women and children.

As for Joseph, he was imprisoned in the Liberty, Missouri, jail for six months. On his return to freedom, it was obvious that his long stay behind bars had heightened his ambitions and his belief in himself. Still searching for the Zion of his dreams, he chose an unpromising, damp area along the Mississippi known as Commerce, Illinois. Its slope upward to its summit gave him a sense of high destiny, however, and he altered its name to Nauvoo, which, he said, (in Hebrew) meant "Beautiful Plantation." Now the vision of a prophet of the Lord, persecuted, imprisoned and released, caught the favor not only of his former followers, but of hundreds of west-going travelers.

There can be no doubt that this young leader of thousands of converts to the religion he had been the first to expound had now begun to read the classics. Though he may well have been the uneducated boy his adherents declared he was, there has never been convincing proof that his education went beyond the modicum provided by the Palmyra schools. But in the years since the Mormon Church had been established, he had become a man of very eager mind. He made strenuous efforts to learn foreign languages. In 1836 he wrote, "My soul delights in reading the word of the Lord in the original and I am determined to pursue the study of the languages until I shall become master of them if I am permitted to live long enough." He was greatly interested in other parts of the world, though, and like many another romantic, his writings showed a strong fascination with disasters such as hurricanes, fires, eruptions of volcanoes. From his speeches, especially those he delivered in Nauvoo, it became evident that he was familiar with some of the works of the great Elizabethans. He even caught inspiration from passages of William Shakespeare and of Christopher Marlowe in his addresses to Mormon audiences:

MARLOWE: Thinkst thou that I who saw the face of God
   And tasted the eternal joys of heaven . . .
SMITH: Shall I who have witnessed the visions of eternity
   and beheld the glorious mansions of bliss . . . Shall I
   who have heard the voice of God and communed with
   angels . . . stoop from the authority of Almighty God.
SHAKESPEARE: You sulphurous and thought-executing fires,
   Vaunt-couriers to oak-cleaving thunderbolts,
   . . . And thou, all-shaking thunder,
   Smite flat the thick rotundity o' the world!
SMITH: Come on ye prosecutors!
   Ye false swearers!
   All hell boil over!
   Ye burning mountains,
   Roll down your lava!
The young Prophet was extremely busy during his

years in Nauvoo. Besides his religious duties as President of the Church, he had become mayor of the town, hotel man, judge, architect, real-estate man. There was scarcely an activity in Nauvoo in which he did not participate.

CHAPTER X

"I Have Unsheathed My Sword"

A sound of talk rose from the east bank of the Mississippi River at Nauvoo on the morning of June 18, 1844. Standing "at ease," the Legion of Nauvoo, fifteen hundred armed and uniformed men, faced the uncompleted wall of a building across the muddy road from Joseph Smith's large new Mansion House. Crowded close behind them, about ten thousand townspeople—men, women, and children—chatted eagerly. Suddenly, sharp commands stiffened the Legion to attention, and silence fell. Trumpets sounded. There was an uneasy shifting as all eyes were fixed on the door of the Mansion House. It opened, and six white-uniformed guards marched briskly from it. Behind them strode their tall Lieutenant General, preceding six more of the guards. Scattered shouts came from the crowd— then long, loud cheering.

From spurs glittering on his shiny black boots to his hat's high crown (gilt stars tossed there among black ostrich plumes), the General was resplendent. Below epaulets on the shoulders of his self-designed blue general's jacket, rows of brass buttons marched to his figured belt, where hung the scabbard of his sword. None of the men about him, not even Porter Rockwell—he of the long curls and burly body—drew the crowd's attention away from the General. A head taller than any of the men in the white circle of his guards, he was the dark champion. The crowd roared its applause as he marched about inspecting his Legion.

It was two o'clock that afternoon before tall young General Smith, Prophet of the Mormons, mayor of the largest city in Illinois, and candidate for the Presidency of the United States, climbed with agility to the top of the unfinished wall. Though his mind was troubled, he resolutely began the speech he already knew might be the last he would ever make to his people. From the towns of Warsaw and Carthage, from the nearby settlements of Ramus, Morley, and Fountain Green, had come riders to report that anti-Mormon mobs were forming. There was already talk of an invasion of Nauvoo that would pit militia companies of the surrounding countryside against the militia in the Legion. During that day and the week that followed, it would seem that only Joseph Smith fully realized the imminence of civil war. Only he was conscious of the deadly intent of his enemies; only he felt the inevitability of tragic consequences.

As the General faced his audience, he was aware that his calling out of the Legion had caused fear and bitterness among non-Mormons in Missouri, Iowa and Illinois. He was still under indictment in Missouri, and he was sure from his recent experiences that the "Pukes" (scornful nickname for Missourians) would not give up trying to extradite, kidnap, or kill him. He knew his order for the destruction of the presses of the Nauvoo *Expositor*, a journal published by rebellious Mormon apostates, had already caused charges of violation of the freedom of the press. He also knew that the paper had justifiably accused him not only of the secret practice of polygamy (of which, according to his confidential report to his closest friends, God's approval had for years been revealed to him) but of urging the Mormon leaders to practice it. His was a desperate situation, but he met it with his usual romantic courage. Always the dramatist, he stood on the unfinished wall and defied his foes with sounding rhetoric and melodramatic gesture.

His speech began simply with a claim of the right of all Mormons to live and be protected from those who threatened them and to receive "the privileges guaranteed by our state and national constitutions."

The volume and intensity of Joseph's voice steadily increased in his next few sentences. After these he paused, and there was deep silence. Then came the deep-voiced utterance of his mighty question:

"Will you all stand by me to the death, and sustain at the peril of your lives the laws of our country, and the liberties and privileges which our fathers have transmitted unto us, sealed with their sacred blood?"

From the men of the Nauvoo Legion and the thousands behind them came a thundering "Aye!"

"It is well," said the Prophet quietly. "If you had not done so, I would have gone out there [he pointed to the west] and raised up a mightier people."

Then he resumed raising his audience to high excitement: "I call upon all men from Maine to the Rocky Mountains and from Mexico to British America whose hearts thrill with horror to behold the rights of free men trampled under foot. . . . Come, all ye lovers of liberty, break the oppressor's rod, loose the iron grasp of mobocracy." From

the scabbard at his side, the General snatched a glittering
blade and raised it above his head.

"I call upon God and angels to witness that I have
unsheathed my sword with a firm and unalterable de-
termination that this people shall have their legal rights . . .
or my blood shall be spilt upon the ground like water,
and my body consigned to the silent tomb. . . . I would
welcome death rather than submit to this oppression; and it
would be sweet, oh sweet, to rest in the grave rather than
to submit."

For an hour more Joseph stirred the emotions of his
people. And in the last minute of his appeal, he trans-
formed himself from soldier in uniform to prophet of
the Lord: "God has tried you. You are a good people;
therefore I love you with all my heart. Greater love hath
no man than that he should lay down his life for his
friends. . . I am willing to sacrifice my life for your
preservation. . . .

"May the Lord God of Israel bless you for ever and
ever. I say it in the name of Jesus Christ of Nazareth and
in the authority of the Holy Priesthood he has conferred
upon me."

As the Prophet-General-Mayor left his makeshift platform, it was obvious to his prominent associates that
he had made the crowning effort of his life. Before the
Legion of Nauvoo, the largest military unit in the frontier
states, he had defied the infuriated mobs still gathering in
the river towns on both sides of the Mississippi. He had
tried to make it clear that he regarded the publishers of the
Expositor as criminals disturbing the peace, as inciters
to violence, and therefore not entitled to federal guaran-
tees of freedom of the press. But he had ignored the fact

that he and the other Mormon leaders had for some time been practicing polygamy. Had he chosen to admit this, the bitterness of the anti-Mormons in the area would unquestionably have brought about an invasion of Nauvoo and civil war.

It is impossible to know how many of Joseph's wives heard his ringing speech that Tuesday afternoon. It would be equally impossible to state definitely how many of the thirty or more women with whom he had gone through marriage ceremonies were "spiritual" wives—wedded to him only "for eternity"—and hence not sharers of his bed. There can be little doubt, however, that among his admiring hearers were several women whom he had married "for time" and with whom he had experienced connubial joys.

Perhaps the most interesting and certainly the most widely known of these was pretty, tiny, blond Lucinda Pendleton Morgan Harris, of whom Joseph had heard much in the days of his upstate New York treasure-digging before he had married his first wife, Emma Hale. Lucinda's first husband had been the William Morgan who had threatened to reveal secrets of the Masons and had been kidnaped and murdered by fanatic members of that fraternity. One of the first of the Prophet's plural wives, Lucinda had, for the seven years since she was thirty, been married to a Mason—George Washington Harris. It was then, living at the Harris home in Far West, Missouri, that Joseph had converted her to acceptance of the plural-marriage principle. Among other spouses (aside from the omnipresent Emma) who may well have listened pridefully to their eloquent husband on that sunny June afternoon in 1844 were twenty-nine-year-old Louisa Beaman, generally thought to be his first plural wife (he had been married to her for three years), and Mary Elizabeth Rollins Lightner, who later reported, "I was sealed to him in the Masonic Hall over the old brick store by Brigham Young in February, 1842."

That same year he had wed Eliza Roxey Snow, poetess, sealed to him in June both for time and eternity; Sarah Anne Whitney, his bride of July; and Elvira Cowles, whom he soon after won for time and eternity. In the spring of 1843 he had added to his mates the Partridge sisters, Elisa, twenty-three, and Emily, nineteen; the Lawrence girls— Mary, twenty, and her sister Sarah, seventeen; Almera Woodward Johnson, thirty-one; Lucy Walker, seventeen; and Olive Frost, twenty-seven. That fall he married nineteen-year-old Melissa Lott, who seems to have been, according to his biographers, the last wife wedded before his murder.

Hence several hearts beat faster as the tall General jumped lightly down from the wall. A black boot reached for a stirrup and a second flashed over the rump of the prancing black stallion, Charlie. As one man, the white-clad dozen of the bodyguard swung into their saddles. In the dark blue uniform, surmounted by the star-sprent plumes, Joseph had become a black eagle floating in a white cloud of doves. The brass band struck up a march, and sharp orders punctuated the music as the officers of the Legion of Nauvoo moved their men into line. Their Lieutenant General and his staff led a great parade up the slanting Main Street toward the unfinished tower of the Temple of the Latter-day Saints, standing lone and high in the rays of the westering sun, while thousands of the Mormon faithful cheered.

After the Legion broke ranks on its parade grounds General Smith rode back to the Mansion House. Messengers had been galloping into town all the afternoon, and they awaited him. They said mobs were forming nearby in the towns of Appanoose and La Harpe, Rocky Run and Green Plains, Pilot Grove and Spilman's Landing. In their opinion, the excited horsemen reported, invasion of Nauvoo was certain. There was even talk of mobs arriving by steamboat at Nauvoo Landing.

After Joseph had gone to bed he was awakened by a persistent knocking on the Mansion House door. When he unbarred and opened, he was just able to recognize in the darkness Shadrach Roundy, a Nauvoo policeman. The officer warned him that a man named Norton had been overheard in the streets making wild threats to shoot him. After some questions and answers, faithful Shadrach resumed his duties, and Joseph went back to bed.

The Legion paraded along the riverbanks every morning in the next few days, and every day the Lieutenant General in full uniform reviewed them. At his order small detachments were constantly galloping over the brown muddy roads that patterned the flat prairie. Pickets were sent out to stand guard on all the approaches to Nauvoo. Families of refugees, driven from their homes by their non-Mormon neighbors, appeared in the streets. A company of the Legion marching from Macedonia to Nauvoo came upon an anti-Mormon unit twice as large as their own, marching under two red flags. These foes at once deployed at the edge of a wood. The Legionnaires "opened file about ten feet apart" and resolutely kept to the road, though under sporadic fire that did no damage.

From widely separated mounds and hillocks the Mormon sentries could see bands of the enemy threading the levels of high grass as they tramped toward Nauvoo.

Lieutenant General Smith, always fascinated by the stratagems of war, frequently rode out on the prairie meadows to survey the situation. He spent much of the rest of his time at his desk in the Mansion House writing suggestions to his outposts that they let the invaders come through and then attack them from the rear, writing orders to distant Mormon communities to send aid, writing to the absent members of the Mormon Council of Twelve informing them of the dangers he faced.

On returning from his review of the Legion on Friday, June 21, General Smith found messengers from the Governor of Illinois, Thomas Ford, who had come to Carthage, eighteen miles distant. He wrote that in the interests of impartial justice "well informed and discreet persons" capable of presenting the Mormon version of recent events should be sent to him. Two representatives were at once appointed, and accompanied by the messengers, they set out for Carthage at seven o'clock and arrived at eleven. John Taylor, one of the two, wrote that "the town was filled with a perfect set of rabble and rowdies" and that they "seemed to be holding a grand saturnalia, whooping, yelling, and vociferating as if bedlam had broken loose."

A meeting the next morning resulted in Governor Ford's stating his desire that General Smith and "all parties concerned in passing or executing the city law in relation to the press" come to Carthage to "allay public excitement" and "prove their wish to be governed by law." Delayed a half day by the Governor's taking time to write a letter to Smith, the messengers were not in Nauvoo until dusk.

Ford's letter was read before a meeting of a few Mormon leaders hastily summoned to an upper room of the Mansion House. Hearts sank as ears heard:

". . . your conduct in the destruction of the press was a very gross outrage upon the laws and liberties of the people. . . . I require any and all of you, who are or shall be accused, to submit yourselves to be arrested. . . . I tell you plainly that if no such submission is made as I have indicated, I will be obliged to call out the militia; and if a few thousand will not be sufficient, many thousands will be. . ."

As the reading ended Joseph said despairingly, "There is no mercy—no mercy here."

He turned to his older brother: "What shall we do?"

"I don't know," said Hyrum.

The Prophet seemed lost in thought. Then his face brightened. "It is clear to my mind what to do," he said. "All they want is Hyrum and myself; then tell everybody to go about their business and not to collect in groups but scatter about. . . . They will come here and search for us. Let them search; they will not harm you in person or property and not even a hair of your head. We will cross the river tonight and go away to the west."

"I told Stephen Markham," wrote Joseph that night in the last entry of his journal, "that if Hyrum and I were ever taken again, we should be massacred, or I was not a prophet of God."

At nine o'clock the door of the Mansion House swung open, and a dim, short ray cut through the darkness.

Hyrum came out, and the light was gone with the sound of the latch.

"A company of men are seeking to kill my brother," said Hyrum to a man standing outside. "The Lord has warned him to flee to the Rocky Mountains to save his life." Without more words the two men waited. Joseph came out suddenly holding a handkerchief to his face. He had said good-by to his Emma, then pregnant, and to their children. He was weeping.

Dark figures had gathered on the riverbank when the brothers came near. The river was higher that June than any old-timer could remember. Someone had gone to borrow a skiff. He had a hard time finding it, and in the long wait Joseph gave directions. "Tell our wives what we calculate to do," he said, "and learn their feelings on the subject; tell Emma that you, Brother Phelps, will take her by the second steamboat upriver to Cincinnati. She has enough money for expenses. If there is anything wrong, come over the river and find out where we are."

It was two o'clock on Sunday morning and raining heavily when the brothers Smith and Willard Richards climbed into the skiff. Following them, Porter Rockwell took the oars and sent it sliding out into the swirling current. Even with his great strength he made slow progress. The boat was flimsy and soon sprang a number of leaks. It was in danger of sinking until the desperate men took off their boots and shoes and used them to bail out the water. The skies were clearing and dawn was spreading behind them when their craft neared the Iowa shore. Mists rose from the river. They seemed to catch in the lush, green foliage and take their color from it. As the sunlight burned them away, the men in the boat could see cabins standing in coffee-colored water so deep that only roofs and chimneys rose above it. As his passengers clambered out on the bank, Porter Rockwell swung the skiff about and rowed back toward the sun-gilded town whence they had come. He had orders to bring back Joseph's best horses in the dark of the following night.

By one o'clock that afternoon, however, the tireless giant had returned, and he was not alone. Three grim emissaries from Nauvoo stalked into Mormon William Jordan's farmhouse where the brothers were packing provisions for a journey to the "Great Basin of the Rocky Mountains." These messengers said the city was leaderless and in a panic. They accused the Prophet of forsaking his people out of sheer cowardice. They said that even his faithful Emma demanded his return. "When the shepherd deserts his sheep," said one of them, "who will save them from the wolves?" The question marked the crisis of the conflict that raged within Joseph. From this moment flight with honor was impossible; death was certain. "If my life is of no value to my friends," he said, as if he could not believe what he had just heard, "it is of none to myself."

The fugitive General turned to Porter Rockwell, symbol of strength. "What shall I do?" he said.

"You're the oldest," said the big man, "you ought to know best. You make your bed. I'll lie with you."

Grasping at this straw of logic, Joseph appealed to his brother: "You are the oldest, Hyrum. What shall we do?"

Said the always-confident Hyrum, "Go back and give ourselves up, and see this thing out."

"If you go back I will go with you," said Joseph, "but we shall be butchered."

[101]

"No, no," said Hyrum, "let us go back and put our trust in God, and we shall not be harmed. The Lord is in it. If we live or have to die, we will be reconciled to our fate."

The decision made, the brothers wrote a letter from "Bank of the River Mississippi" to Governor Ford in Carthage. It said they would come to Carthage the next day, and it asked for protection by a posse, which they would meet at "the Mound" outside the town about two o'clock in the afternoon.

They recrossed the still flooding river at dusk. As they approached Nauvoo Landing Joseph, remembering the day of the week, said softly, "I wish I could preach to the Saints once more," and the oarsman, Rockwell, looking up at the deepening blue above him, said, "We could tell everybody and they could listen by starlight."

There was no meeting of the Saints that night. For the General there were preparations to be made, messages to be sent, orders to be given, farewells to be said. There was no time for a prophet to foretell his doom to his people at the hushed grove under the stars.

CHAPTER XI

Last Days of a Prophet

Joseph rose early the next morning and rode with friends up to the Temple. The hammers of builders had not yet begun their clangor. Only in his imaginings could he see the high white spire he had planned. Sitting easily in his saddle, he looked down the hill at his waking town. "This is the loveliest place and the best people under the heavens," he said. "Little do they know the trials that await them."

The little band trotted along the Carthage road, and the warm, wet smell of the prairie was around them. Goldfinches flitted ahead of them, constantly arching the limitless levels. Horned meadow larks sang beside them, and the air was sweet with the song of the white-throated sparrow. Close to the earth puccoons, paintbrush and windflowers gave pastel underlining to grasses as high as the horses' stirrups. Looking at the little band, an artist might well have likened them to horsemen caught for an instant on the minted surface of a golden tapestry.

They had traveled about twelve miles and the Mound loomed ahead, when they saw sweeping toward them a long line of uniformed troopers. Outnumbered by almost three to one, the Mormons halted in a close-knit, fearful bundle. Said their commander: "Do not be alarmed, brothers, for they cannot do more to you than the enemies of truth did to the ancient Saints—they can only kill the body."

The strangers halted, and their captain came forward to present an order from Governor Ford which required the Legion of Nauvoo to surrender all state-owned arms to him. Joseph countersigned it and ordered a deputy to hurry back to Nauvoo and inform the Legion officers it must be complied with immediately.

As he watched his messenger gallop away, Joseph said: "I am going like a lamb to the slaughter; but I am calm as a summer morning. I have a conscience void of offense towards God and towards all men. I shall die innocent and it shall be said of me, 'He was murdered in cold blood.' "

A few moments later, however, at the urgent request of the troopers' captain, General Smith decided to return to the city to aid in the execution of the order. Some of the Mormon company rode on to Carthage. The rest began with him the long ride back home. When they reached Nauvoo the Legionnaires were already bringing their weapons to the Masonic Hall. During his wait for completion of the order Joseph twice rode to the Mansion House to say good-by to his family. All arms had been delivered before six o'clock, when the final journey to Carthage began. As he passed his farm on the edge of the town, Joseph stopped to look at it.

It was nearly July, but his corn, drowned out early by heavy showers and then replanted, was short. He watched it climbing green from the wet earth into late afternoon sunlight while about fifteen riders gradually assembled about him. Then his long hands tightened on his rein.

"If some of you had such a farm and knew you would not see it any more," he said, "you would want to take a good look at it for the last time." After these words he and his silent companions rode off into the swift-settling dusk.

It was ten o'clock when they were back at the Mound. There they stopped at a farmhouse to eat and drink the refreshments they had brought from home in their saddlebags. The troopers who had received the Legion's arms caught up with them here. They would act as guards for the Mormons as they entered Carthage. Guards were needed, for the town was in a wild uproar. It was midnight as the procession reached the square where the town's militia, the Carthage Grays, awaited it. The tired escort slumped in their saddles as they rode wearily by with their even more exhausted prisoners placed for safety inside their columns.

From the crowd in the square came drunken cries of derision and hatred: "Where's the damn' Prophet?" "Clear the way and show us Joe Smith, Prophet of God." "God damn you, old Joe, we've got you now!"

The column stopped before the Hamilton House, and the jeering of the crowd increased. A second-story window rose with a sharp crack.

"Gentlemen," said the high, thin voice of the Governor of Illinois, "I know your anxiety to see Mr. Smith, which is natural enough, but it is quite too late tonight for you to have that opportunity; but I assure you, gentlemen, you shall have that privilege tomorrow morning, as I will cause him to pass before the troops upon the square, and

[105]

now I wish you, with this assurance, quietly and peacefully to return to your quarters."

The window closed, and the crowd wandered away, while the hotel hostlers led the horses of the guests to the barn.

On the next morning, the Governor made good his promise. He issued an early order calling upon all troops in Carthage to assemble near the courthouse, and there to form a hollow square. In the meantime Joseph and Hyrum were put under arrest on a new charge, that of treason against the state of Illinois for having called out the Mormon militia unit—the Legion of Nauvoo—in the previous week.

At a little before ten o'clock the Governor climbed on an old table in the middle of the formation and appealed for order and correct behavior. Then the officer in command of the troops, General Deming, and Joseph and Hyrum Smith entered the square. Leading the way, Governor Ford introduced the brothers as "General Joseph Smith" and "General Hyrum Smith." The Carthage Grays yelled loud protest. Their officers threw their hats in the air, drew their swords, yelled profane epithets at the Mormons. The Governor remonstrated with them politely and with the aid of General Deming quieted the demonstration.

The rest of the day was spent at the Hamilton House in legal arguments between the Mormons, the Governor, and Carthage local authorities. It ended, despite bitter protests, in the Mormon generals and several of their Mormon friends being escorted, "for their security," by a militia detachment to the Carthage jail.

The jail was a sturdy two-story building. Its walls were

of stone, and its hand-hewn oak beams were heavy and strong. A wooden staircase led from the first floor, which contained the jailer's quarters, to cells above and one large, unbarred, informal chamber which held a bed and chairs. The two generals, accompanied by five of their Mormon friends (against whom no charges had been lodged), found this the most suitable room for the group. The jailer made other rooms available, and all were treated with courtesy. They found the conversation on that Tuesday night "amusing," and they were all in better spirits as they stretched themselves on the wide floor boards to sleep.

On the morning of Wednesday, the twenty-sixth, Governor Ford came to the jail, and he and Joseph had a long debate on the issues involved in the charges. Ford proved to be a stickler for the law as he interpreted it, and Joseph's efforts to persuade him that the orders for the destruction of the *Nauvoo Expositor* press and the calling out of the Legion to establish martial law were in the interests of the public safety, made little impression. The Governor left, and Joseph devoted the next few hours to correspondence.

In the afternoon a constable came to the jail and demanded custody of the brothers that he might take them to court for a hearing. The jailer refused to give them up, but the constable came back soon with a detail of the Carthage Grays, who were so threatening that Joseph and Hyrum were once more ordered into the streets. A wild and vociferous crowd greeted them, but the brothers moved swiftly into the midst of it and, locking arms with the most virulent of their enemies, made their way to the courthouse. The humiliation of being displayed before thousands of spectators as if they were animals in a traveling show ("like elephants," as one eyewitness expressed it) was in marked contrast with the honor accorded them in much larger Nauvoo only a few miles away—a fact that both they and their enemies could not have failed to note.

After futile arguments before Justice Robert F. Smith, who was also a captain of the Carthage Grays, the prisoners were returned to the jail. After they had left the court, Justice Smith, whose purposes were by now unquestionably criminal, set the date of trial for the twenty-ninth, in order, he said, that he might accompany his command on an official visit to Nauvoo ordered by Governor Ford for the next day.

After their supper the brothers and the companions who were with them in the large upstairs room heard Hyrum Smith read from the *Book of Mormon* narratives of the deliverance from prison of devout believers in Christ. It was obvious that all seven had been shaken by the malignancy of the crowds through which they had just passed. Joseph in particular was downcast. He had been able to read the intent to murder in the eyes and attitudes of the enraged soldiers and citizenry, and the confidence that had served him in many an incident involving danger to himself had deserted him. Though he had often been attacked by his enemies, he had emerged time and again as master of a seemingly hopeless situation. Now he felt only a growing sense of danger.

Willard Richards sat up late after the others had lain down to sleep. By the light of a tallow candle he was copying papers he regarded as essential to a true summary of the events of the week. The long bodies of the Prophet and his brother lay on the bedstead. The others slept on mattresses laid on the floor. At midnight the candle began to gutter. Suddenly in the darkness outside, but very close, a gun spoke sharply. The echo was still sounding as the sleeping men woke, startled and dismayed. It was hard, in the ensuing quiet, to go back to sleep.

Joseph rose from the bed and lay down on a mattress. "Lay your head on my arm for a pillow, Brother John," he said. Then the other men, unable to sleep, heard him talking softly of his feeling that death was on its way.

"I would like to see my family again," he said. And, after a moment of silence, "Would to God I could preach to the Saints in Nauvoo once more." Later the sleepless six men heard the Prophet's voice in the darkness: "Are you afraid to die?"

A different voice from the mattress said: "Has that time come? In such a cause, I do not think death would have many terrors." Silence and darkness then—and as light began, the atmosphere was dull and heavy. A shower rattled on the roof.

On that dawn—the morning of June twenty-seventh—a company of Warsaw militia under Colonel Levi Williams set out to march from their home town to Nauvoo, according to the Governor's orders. They had covered about eight miles when a courier came galloping across the prairie. He gave the Colonel an order from Governor Ford to disband his troops. The communication also said that the Governor himself, on his way to Nauvoo, was countermanding his order for the Warsaw men to meet him at Golden Point, as previously arranged. His guard into the Mormon city would include the Carthage Grays, except for a detachment of some fifty selected members of the company who had been left behind to guard the prisoners in the jail.

Loud protests came from the Warsaw troops. They were "loaded for bear," they said, and had no intention of going back home. Incited further by their captains, many volunteered to march to Carthage. At this moment another messenger dashed up. He wore the uniform of the Carthage Grays. What his orders were has never been discovered, but the events of the day provided clues. An article in the *Atlantic Monthly* for December, 1867, by the distinguished John Hay, later a biographer of Abraham Lincoln and member of the Presidential Cabinet from 1898 to 1905, tells what its author learned from his father (who obeyed the order to go back to Warsaw) and from other dependable sources.

The Warsaw militia were "annoyed at the prospect of their picnic coming so readily to an end, at losing the fun of sacking Nauvoo, at having to go home without material for a single romance." A hundred and fifty started on the march to Carthage, but the heat and humidity of the day caused that number to dwindle to seventy-five and put those who persevered in a murderous mood. Sweating and purposeful, they sang an adaptation of an old marching song as they plodded along. To the tune of "Where Now Are the Hebrew Children?" they howled out,

Where now is the Prophet Joseph
Where now is the Prophet Joseph
Where now is the Prophet Joseph
Safe, safe in the Carthage jail.

While the Warsaw men were marching on the prairie, ominous events were making the Carthage jail seem far from safe. One by one the Mormon friends of the Prophet Joseph and his brother were being separated from them. One, Dan Jones, went outside to discover what he could about the temper of the town. He became so alarmed at the talk of killing that he hurried to the Governor to tell him of the possibility of a lynching. He found Ford at the point of starting his ride to Nauvoo. Excitedly he told his story. Said Thomas Ford coldly, "You are unnecessarily alarmed for the safety of your friends, sir; the people are not that cruel." When Dan ran back to report, the guards at the jail refused him admittance.

After Dan had left the jail, Joseph wrote what proved to be his last letter to Emma. Whatever other loyalties he had, it was always to her that he turned in time of serious trouble.

Dear Emma [he wrote]: The Governor continues his courtesies and permits us to see our friends. We hear this morning that the Governor will not go down with his troops today to Nauvoo as anticipated last evening; but if he does come down with his troops you will be protected. . . . There is no danger of an exterminating order. . . .

There is one principle which is eternal: It is the duty of all men to protect their lives and the lives of their household, whenever necessity requires, and no power has the right to forbid it, should the last extreme arrive; but I anticipate no such extreme, but caution is the parent of safety.

Joseph Smith

P.S. Dear Emma, I am very much resigned to my lot, knowing I am justified and have done the best that could be done. Give my love to the children and all my friends . . . as for treason—I know that I have not committed any, and they cannot prove an appearance of anything of the kind, so you need not have any fears that anything can happen to us on that score. May God bless you all. Amen.

A Mormon friend, Cyrus Wheelock, obtained a pass from the Governor early that morning. During a shower he put on his overcoat and went to the jail. On the strength of the pass, the guards allowed him to enter without searching him. Joseph ordered Wheelock to ride to Nauvoo with orders to the Legion to refrain from any military display and to the people to stay indoors and not to gather in groups while the Governor and his military escort were there. Before Wheelock left, he took from under the overcoat, where he had concealed it, a six-shooter of the sort then popularly known as an "Allen's pepperbox" and secretly placed it in Joseph's pocket. Joseph then turned over to Hyrum a pistol with a single barrel which had also been smuggled into the jail by a Mormon friend.

After eating his noon meal that day Willard Richards, understandably nervous from the tension growing both outside and inside the jail, complained of feeling ill. Joseph asked another of his Mormon companions to get something for Richards that "would settle his stomach." Engaged on that errand, the friend was surrounded by members of the Carthage street mob and forced to ride out of town. Now besides Joseph and Hyrum there were only two men left in the big upstairs room—Willard Richards, a big, wide-faced New England doctor, a year older than Joseph, who had joined the church at Kirtland, where he was baptized by his cousin, Brigham Young; and John Taylor, of English birth, a slight man of thirty-six. Both were members of the Council of the Twelve Apostles, all others being absent on important missions.

As the afternoon wore on, its heat and the dampness of the air increased. The men lounged near the open windows in their shirt sleeves. Little was said. The jailer, probably more aware than his charges of the waiting mood of the silent little town, came in to suggest that they might be safer in the small locked cells. Joseph said they would enter them after supper. He said to Willard Richards, "If we go into the cell, will you go with us?"

Richards replied, "Brother Joseph, you did not ask me to cross the river with you—you did not ask me to come to Carthage—you did not ask me to come to jail with you —and do you think I would forsake you now? But I will tell you what I will do; if you are condemned to be hung for treason, I will be hung in your stead, and you shall go free."

Joseph said, "You cannot."

"I will," said his friend.

Then Joseph asked John Taylor to sing for him a religious ballad that had recently become popular in Nauvoo —"A Poor Wayfaring Man of Grief." The song had been written by a Scottish hymn writer, James Montgomery, in 1826 before Joseph had climbed Hill Cumorah to take away the golden plates, and it was possible that he had known it for a number of years after that. It held fourteen stanzas, and Taylor did not omit any of them. Six of them summarize its story and meaning:

A poor wayfaring man of grief
  Had often crossed me on my way,
Who sued so humbly for relief
  That I could never answer, Nay.

I spied him where a fountain burst
  Clear from the rock—his strength was gone.

The heedless water mock'd his thirst,
   He heard it, saw it hurrying on.

I ran and rais'd the suff'rer up;
   Thrice from the stream he drain'd my cup,
Dipp'd, and returned it running o'er;
   I drank and never thirsted more.

In pris'n I saw him next—condemned
   To meet a traitor's doom at morn;
The tide of lying tongues I stemmed,
   And honored him 'mid shame and scorn.

My friendship's utmost zeal to try,
   He asked if I for him would die;
The flesh was weak, my blood ran chill;
   But the free spirit cried, "I will!"

Then in a moment to my view,
   The stranger stated from disguise;
The tokens in his hands I knew,
   The Saviour stood before mine eyes.

The tune to which these verses were set was melancholy, but the image of the poor wayfaring man had ever been one which moved the Prophet deeply, and as John Taylor sang, he must have remembered the three wandering Nephites described in the *Book of Mormon*. The hot, quiet building echoed to his mellow voice, and there was a long silence when he stopped singing. Then Hyrum asked him to sing the long hymn again. John Taylor said despondently, "I do not feel like singing," but he began again.

While the song was coming from the jailhouse, young Billy Hamilton, son of the owner of the Hamilton House, stood in the cupola of the courthouse watching with a large field glass the west road into Carthage. At about four o'clock he saw a large number of men gathered beyond a point of woods about two miles away. Fifteen minutes later they began to move toward the town in single file and at a quick pace. They used a rail fence as a partial screen, and they carried guns at the trail as if they were trying to hide them. Billy raced down the steps from the cupola and ran toward the jail. By the time he reached it, the awaited crime had been committed.

John Taylor had hardly completed the long ballad for the second time when he saw from an open front window a number of men with painted faces come around the corner of the jail. They made for the stairs, and the four men above heard a sharp volley and the leaden thud of bullets in the wooden wall beyond the landing. There was a swift pounding of feet on the steps. Taylor ran to the door of the room but found the big strong torsos of Hyrum and Willard Richards braced against it. A shot from the other side broke the weak latch and Hyrum and Willard backed away. As they did so, a bullet through the door hit Hyrum in the face. At the same time, a shot fired through the open window struck him in the side.

"I am a dead man," said Hyrum in a strangely emphatic voice, and he fell on his back.

Joseph leaned over the dead body. "O my poor dear brother Hyrum!" he said. Then he moved swiftly to the door, opened it a few inches, and aimed the pepperbox six-shooter down the hall. Three times it failed him; three times it fired. Cries of anguish told him the bullets had hit his targets. The long rifles of the mob were moving through the crack in the door now. It opened wider, and the besieged men saw the blackened faces of the murderers. The mob-men snarled and held back as they saw the big man in front of them, but the crowd behind was pushing them inexorably forward. They fired, and as they did so, John Taylor grabbed the stout walking stick which one of their Mormon visitors had left behind (a "rascal beater," he had called it) and knocked down the muzzles of their guns. "That's right, Brother Taylor," said Joseph, "parry them off as well as you can."

More guns appeared in the doorway, and the men behind them screamed their hatred as they tried to angle their fire toward the Mormons. At last the murderers were inside, and John Taylor made for the window in the hope of jumping out and taking a chance on escape from the yard below. As he threw himself toward the opening, a bullet hit him in the thigh. He would have fallen outside, however, had not another shot, which shattered the watch in his vest, knocked him back into the room. Almost unconscious, he still had presence of mind enough to roll under the bedstead. Now Joseph made his try at the window. He was almost out when two bullets from the doorway ripped into his body and another pierced his right breast.

"O Lord," said the Prophet loudly, "My God," and as he spoke he went out feet first through the window. The long body fell heavily into the yard beside the well.

"He's leaped the window," came a voice from the jail, and the men who had been upstairs raced down to the yard. One of them bent over him. At the words, "He's dead," the black-faced murderers cheered lustily. Then there was silence. Already a number of them were running away. Someone said, "The Mormons are coming," and there was a scramble to run out of sight into the woods from which they had begun their attack.

Willard Richards, who had been behind the door when it was forced open and had not been noticed by the mob, started for the cells on the other side of the second floor. "Take me," said John Taylor, and Richards lifted his desperately wounded friend and bore him to a cell where he laid him on the floor and covered him with a straw mattress that had burst its seams.

A few of the bolder members of the mob raced up the stairs once more and stood for a moment looking at the corpse of Hyrum. They did not look in the cells, but ran down to catch up with their fleeing accomplices.

Richards waited beside John Taylor until he was sure they had gone. Then he went slowly down into the yard. He bent over the murdered Prophet and somehow swung the tall man into his arms, then over his shoulders. Step by step he staggered up the stairs again, and when he had come into the big room, he laid the body of the Prophet Joseph beside that of his brother.

CHAPTER XII

"My Body Consigned to the Silent Tomb"

Suddenly the jail which less than five minutes before had been crowded with sweating, swearing men stood lonely in deepening dusk. Inside the gaping upper window through which Joseph had fallen an opaque darkness had already enveloped the bodies of the dead brothers. A lamp shone in the window of jailer Stigall's quarters on the first floor and from that direction came the sound of crying children.

The voice of Stigall himself, pleading for help from a young country doctor who had walked down the muddy street to find out what the shots had meant, was high-pitched and strained. Mormon John Taylor, he said, was still alive though bleeding from many wounds.

More than fifty years later Dr. Thomas L. Barnes wrote at the request of a daughter what he remembered of his few minutes with Taylor after he had granted Stigall's request:

> We found him in a pile of straw. He was very frightened as well as severely wounded. It took strong persuading of the jailer as well as our positive assurance that we meant him no harm but were desirous of doing him some good.

He finally consented to come out of his cell. When we examined him we had found that he had been hit by four balls. . . . The wounds had bled quite freely, the blood had had time to coagulate, which it had done, and where the clothes and straw came in contact they all adhered together so that . . . he was a pitiable looking sight. We took the best care of him we could till he left us.

At five minutes after eight Willard Richards, after the most dangerous and sorrowful hours of his life, rested his big body on a jail chair and wrote a message to Nauvoo.

Joseph and Hyrum are dead, Taylor wounded, not very badly. Our guard was forced, as we believe by a band of Missourians from 100 to 200. The job was done in an instant, and the party fled toward Nauvoo instantly. This is as I believe it. The citizens here are afraid of the Mormons' attacking them; I promise them no.

Willard Richards

John Taylor signed an added sentence:

The citizens promise us protection; alarm guns have been fired.

The guns had resounded through streets of empty houses. Terrified, the people of Carthage had fled into the prairie. Richards had difficulty in finding men to move the corpses to the Hamilton House and to build there the pine boxes in which they would be transported to Nauvoo. The coroner's jury, hastily summoned, had hurried through their duties and raced away. Fear that the Nauvoo Legion was already riding on a vengeful mission scattered wagons filled with Carthage families over the broad level land. They had left doors and windows open as they deserted their homes. Lightnings in the starless, moonless sky and gusts of rain only added to their fears. No lamps burned on the prairie farms that night though houses and barns alike were crowded with stricken people. Some of them may have heard hoofbeats outside for Sam Smith, younger brother of Joseph and Hyrum, was making his way through the blackness toward Carthage. On a lather-streaked horse he loped swiftly into the town, there to tell Willard Richards he had set out to visit his brothers hours before but had met a mob of anti-Mormons who, on finding out who he was, threatened to kill him. He had spurred his horse suddenly and the animal had leaped away from his captors and outrun their pursuit.

Dr. Barnes had volunteered to persuade a messenger to take the short message from Richards and Taylor to Nauvoo. In the hours thereafter no one whom he asked would face the peril of being captured, perhaps murdered, by partisans he might meet in the wet darkness of the eighteen-mile stretch of prairie. At last toward morning one Arza Adams, aided by a guide who knew every detail of the landscape, made the ride over a "blind road" only to discover as he entered town at sunrise that Nauvoo had received the news before midnight.

In Carthage the hammering on the boxes had stopped before the light of a moist gray morning began to spread. Billy Hamilton, after an evening of closing windows and doors, had helped with the collecting and hiding of the town's official papers lest Mormons seize them after a sudden attack. Now he was up after little sleep and had hitched a team of horses to each of the two wagons which would bear the pine coffins and their pitiful cargo to Nauvoo.

The day was of the sort that legends follow. It brought with it no sunrise, and the gray bowl above the prairie was filled with wind-driven clouds. Thunder muttered on the edges of the world and occasional lightnings flashed crookedly into the sky like outer flames of a conflagration for the most part out of sight.

There had been no time to make covers for the boxes and they lay open in front of the hotel. The corpses lay in them, stiffened into grotesque positions. A squad of eight uniformed horsemen, ordered by the commanding general of the State of Illinois militia, waited indolently by the wagons.

As the cortege began to form, a bright ray shot through the clouds. Members of the party gathered green shrubs and branches of trees which they spread over the bodies to shield them if the sun were to come out hot, and Mr. Hamilton spread a worn Indian blanket above the greenery that covered Joseph's body. Though the tavern keeper's son begged permission to go along, his father emphatically refused it.

Slowly, then, at eight o'clock, the long journey began. The drivers of the teams were Samuel Smith, overtired and already beginning to show evidence of the illness which would end his life a month later, and Mr. Hamilton. A militiaman rode at each wheel, and Willard Richards, a heavy burden for any mount, trotted about as earnest supervisor. About two miles out of Carthage came a slow ascent on the eastern side of the Mound—then the slanting return to the level of the plain. Continuous rains during the week had left the road rough and muddy. On both sides of it lay pools of water from which thick swales of tall grass pushed upward. Over the lush land blew the damp breezes of summer, bringing with them the almost stifling smell of the prairie.

Two miles more, and the wagons were jolting past farmer Fellow's house where Joseph, Hyrum, and the cavalcade of their friends had stopped four days before for a jolly evening snack from the food in their saddlebags.

The soldier guards lounged in their saddles, relieved that they saw no groups of horsemen ahead. Mr. Hamilton drove stolidly as his horses lessened the distance to the Mississippi. But storms of grief assailed the minds of Sam Smith and Willard Richards.

Afternoon, warm and heavy, had come before the party could see, on a hilltop, the unfinished spire of the Nauvoo Temple. It was more than an hour later that they became aware of an unidentifiable sound in the air. It grew louder as the lumbering wagons rolled nearer to Nauvoo. When they turned left on Mulholland Street it had grown to a volume and a quality nearly intolerable. A multitude from the houses of Nauvoo were walking toward the little procession.

The sound was a composite of measureless cries of sorrow. Swelling and receding, it was a vast ululation of lament. In the preceding months the steam packets of the Mississippi had brought up from New Orleans to the Nauvoo docks hundreds of families who had been converted by Mormon missionaries in the British Isles. Faith in the inspiration of the Prophet whom the Americans had praised with song and text had led them to leave their homes and travel to Nauvoo, City of Zion on America's western frontier. Here they had felt assurance in the kindly presence of their Prophet. Now he was dead. The high-voiced keening of the Irish rose above the deep-toned wailing of the Welch and the sobbing of those whose homes had been in the shires of England. No one in America had ever heard such a sound. No one would ever hear its like again.

As the crowd reached the creaking wagons it turned back upon itself and surged slowly toward the river. Gravely the eleven men of the rude cortege kept up the slow rhythm of their progress down the slant of the hill. When the boxes had been carried into the Mansion House the crowd gathered beside the unfinished Nauvoo House across the way to hear Willard Richards describe, from the very platform on which the Prophet had defied his enemies, the tragedy at Carthage. Inside the house three Mormons whose experiences had inured them to the sight and smell of blood were washing the stiff corpses. Once the task was ended, they placed camphor-soaked cotton in each wound, then laid out the bodies "with fine plain drawers and shirt, white neckerchiefs, white cotton stockings and white shrouds."

Now the door to the room opened to reveal Emma Smith waiting with her children. At sight of her dead husband she screamed and nearly fell. A friend stepped to her side and supported her. Violently then, she threw herself forward. "My husband, my husband," she said in a breaking voice. "They have taken you from me at last." She bent to kiss the dead man's lips. "Joseph," she cried, "speak to me." Behind her, calm and reserved, Mary Smith stood silent, looking down on the mutilated face of her Hyrum.

The night of June 28 was sleepless for the mourning

[123]

city. As if sensing the horror that numbed the minds of their owners, dogs howled and cattle bellowed restlessly. Mormon riders sifted into Nauvoo past the whispering sentinels who were guarding the city against marauders still galloping the dark prairie.

The eastern light broke dim on the half-built spire of the temple. A crowd was forming beside the Mansion House down by the river. At seven the door swung open on the shrouded dead. They lay in white-lined walnut coffins which had been covered with black velvet and encased in the white pine boxes. All day Mormons—about ten thousand of them—shuffled through the room, peering through brass-hinged glass lids for a dim last view of the faces of their Prophet and his brother.

B. W. Richmond, a non-Mormon hotel guest, watched the procession for a while. A short, slight woman, he observed, was standing where she could look through the glass above Joseph's head and weeping convulsively. Since no revelation on polygamy was yet generally known, it is probable that few if any of the slow-moving throng could have identified her as an early bride in Joseph's series of plural marriages. Blond, blue-eyed Lucinda Morgan Harris Smith was for the second time sobbing over the corpse of a husband murdered by fanatics.

The doors of the Mansion House were shut at five. A dreary light was waning as the pine boxes were lifted into a hearse. Funeral services had already begun in the grove near the temple as the plodding horses drew the boxes out Mulholland Street toward the city cemetery. Only a few of the sorrowing crowd knew that when the boxes were lowered into newly dug graves, no bodies were in them. Only sandbags gave them weight other than their own.

The velvet-wrapped coffins had been sealed with brass nails and kept inside the Mansion House. The Mormon leaders were still so fearful that there would be attempts to steal the bodies that they had performed the complete funeral service over the weighted boxes lest ghouls might rob the graves.

It was not until midnight that ten men left the Mansion House carrying the sable coffins. A lone guard, James Emmet, led the way, his loaded rifle over his shoulder. The pallbearers followed close behind, for the night was as dark as the burdens they carried. Through the garden and around the pump they moved in slow-stepping unison, thence across the road to the open basement of Nauvoo House. There, in ground below the makeshift platform from which Joseph had less than a week before spoken to his people, the group began to dig in the rain-soaked earth. Piles of soil grew behind them. The spades had soon dug cavities of sufficient depth. Hastily the diggers lowered the coffins, then covered them. They carried the remaining earth to the river. Carefully they gathered bits of stone and wood that had been left by the men who were erecting Nauvoo House and dropped them over the graves to make the broken surface look like the carelessly strewn adjacent ground. Then they hurried home. Soon in their beds they heard on their roofs the first heavy drops of a rainstorm. Suddenly a deluge was pounding the town—destroying all footprints, all other vestiges of their night's labors. The bodies of Joseph and Hyrum would be safe now. The watery mud had covered their black velvet wrappings and gave no evidence of what lay beneath.

In the aftermath of the stunning disaster, the Mormon city quietly but fearfully awaited its future. In a few days John Taylor began his journey in a wagon provided by devoted Mormon friends. His four wounds caused him such agony that he was eventually placed in a sleigh which was dragged over the wet swale beside the road all the way to Nauvoo. There he was received with tenderness and enthusiastic acclaim.

Hatred continued to spread throughout the Carthage-Hancock-Nauvoo triangle on the prairie. The Mormons who had accompanied John Taylor brought the wild folksay that grows out of tense emotions and wish-laden antagonisms. One report went that as Joseph's body lay beside the well in the jailyard, a fiend in blackface flourished a knife with the intent of cutting off its head. As the ghoul raised the blade, however, a bolt of lightning streaked down from the clouds and paralyzed his hand. Another incredible rumor reported that a boy of the Warsaw military band dashed out from the mob and began beating his pewter fife on the head of the corpse while screaming that the Prophet had "ruined" his father.

Soon a news journal from Quincy, Illinois, appeared in Nauvoo: "The money-digger, the juggler, and the founder of the Golden Bible delusion, has been hurried away in the midst of his madness to his final account . . ."

It was fortunate for the Mormons on the Mississippi that their Prophet had realized his danger some weeks before his death. At that time when only John Taylor and Willard Richards of the Council of the Twelve were near him, he sent urgent word to the absent members who were on missions in eastern states to come back to Nauvoo at once.

"My Body Consigned to the Silent Tomb"

Brigham Young entered into his journal after his return that on the evening of the day of murders he was sitting in the railroad depot in Boston waiting for a train to Salem. "I felt a heavy depression of Spirit," he wrote, "and so melancholy I could not converse with any degree of pleasure. Not knowing anything concerning the tragedy enacting at this time in Carthage jail I could not assign my reasons for my peculiar feelings."

On a west-bound Erie Canal packet during that fateful twilight hour, Parley P. Pratt later testified that he and his brother William were talking on deck when "a strange and silent awe, as if the powers of hell were let loose," came over him. He described this feeling at some length to his brother and exclaimed, "O, how sensible I am of the Spirit of murder which seems to pervade the whole land."

CHAPTER XIII

The Mormon Trail

After the secret midnight burial at Nauvoo of Prophet Joseph Smith and his elder brother Hyrum, and their sham public funeral, there was great contention among the Latter-day Saints as to who would become their President. At a vast meeting beside the unfinished temple on August 8, 1844, Sidney Rigdon urged from a wagon before the stand in the grove that he be made Church Guardian, claiming that he had received a revelation from on high that this should be his office.

A little later, a sturdy figure rose from the audience and spoke for himself. Not as tall as Joseph Smith, Brigham Young was nevertheless of commanding presence. He proclaimed himself a dedicated follower of the Prophet and he spoke with a sincerity and practicality that made Rigdon seem both small and pretentious. He was overwhelmingly sustained as President of the "Twelve Apostles," on whom the power of the church now rested.

Brigham Young had been born four years earlier than Joseph Smith, and also in the state of Vermont. His family had moved to Western New York when he was two. According to his later account, he and his lifelong friend and fellow Mormon, Heber C. Kimball, grew up together in the town of Mendon (a scant fifteen miles from the home of Joseph Smith). Here in their early years they busied themselves "picking up brush, dropping down trees, rolling logs . . . and getting our shins, feet and toes bruised." As he grew older Brigham devoted his energies to becoming a carpenter and joiner. There are fine houses still standing in New York State (including the home of Lincoln's Secretary of State, William Henry Seward, at Auburn) that are testimonials to the thoroughness and quality of his craftsmanship.

The young builder was converted to the Church of Jesus Christ of Latter-day Saints by Mormon neighbors. He did not meet the founder of the faith until 1832, after Joseph had moved to Kirtland, Ohio. At that time Brigham made a pilgrimage for the express purpose of declaring his loyalty and found Joseph in the forest, back of the house where he was living, "chopping and hauling wood." Thus the originator of the Mormon Church and the man who was to do more than any other member in perpetuating it, both Yankee born, became known to each other.

The new head of the Latter-day Saints was to prove himself not only an effective administrative officer but one of the greatest leaders of men in all American history. He spoke the vernacular of his time with exactness of meaning, with occasional storms of emphasis, and with a homely but imaginative poetry. He had an intuitive knowledge of his fellows. He had common sense. He had a kind of down-to-earth spirituality. And he bristled with authority.

Though Brigham Young was aware of the gathering tempest of hatred that was soon to result in the Mormons being driven out of Nauvoo by armed mobs, he and his associates insisted that the magnificent temple of which Joseph Smith had dreamed be completed. Before it was finished, however, the decision had been made that the whole body of the Nauvoo Saints would move westward. The first wagons left Nauvoo in February, 1846.

On the journey to Winter Quarters William Clayton wrote the stanzas to a poem and entitled it *All Is Well*, but it soon attained the more appropriate title which it now bears, "Come, Come Ye Saints." No one, neither Mormon nor non-Mormon should miss hearing the 375-voice Mormon choir sing it. The music for this most famous and impressive of all Mormon hymns was derived from an English folk song, "Good Morning Gossip Joan," which Virginia scholars have discovered in rural Virginia areas as "Good Morning Neighbor Jones." It is surprising, therefore, to come upon it as the stately and glorious hymn that it really is.

Several thousand Mormons had arrived at the Missouri River near Council Bluffs by mid-June. At the end of the month they received a request from President Polk that they provide a battalion of five hundred recruits for service in the war against Mexico. The troops were furnished immediately, but on account of the loss of these men it was impossible for the migration to continue.

Twelve to fifteen thousand of the Saints settled on the west bank of the Missouri. They planned a temporary city called Winter Quarters, which consisted of more than seven hundred houses mostly made of logs. While they waited at this place (now Florence, a suburb of Council Bluffs), they received word that the few remaining Mormons at Nauvoo had in September been attacked by mobs and after a gallant defense had been driven from the city. A month later, on October 9, vandals burned the temple to the ground. As the winter of 1846–47 set in, Brother Brigham and his advisers planned an exploratory expedition that would set out to find a home for the Mormons in the far west.

He first decided to enlist twelve groups of twelve men each but the number fluctuated as the months went by. At the Church Conference on December 24, 1847, he was upheld as President of the Church and a dozen of the most important Saints were named members of the Council of the Twelve Apostles—among them both Willard Richards and John Taylor, who had been eyewitnesses to the lynching of Prophet Joseph Smith and his brother Hyrum. There were several frustrating delays during the next four months while the wagons gathered and the members of the pioneer band reported. By Saturday, April 10, sixty-four wagons were rolling toward the banks of the Little Elkhorn River, thirty-four miles from Winter Quarters. They crossed Papillion Creek and, as one of the pioneers, Norton Jacobs, recorded their journey, "Towards evening we hove into sight of the Elkhorn River and the valley of the great Platte, affording a full view of the river as it stretched away for many miles to the west." On Sunday morning all wagons were ferried across the Elkhorn and were counted as sixty-nine. Still there were delays, occasioned by necessary rides back to Winter Quarters for conferences, for more good-bys to families, for brothers who were hurrying from eastern places. On April 14, William Clayton at his home in Winter Quarters was suddenly told by Brigham Young and Willard Richards "to rise up and start with the pioneers in half an hours notice." He camped nineteen miles out on the prairie that night, failing to reach the main camp where the pioneers ate a supper of fried catfish, pork and beans, shortcake, milk, and honeycomb.

At eight o'clock on the morning of Friday the sixteenth, President Young had the camp called together at his wagon and ordered a count of those going on the journey. There were 143 men, three women, and two children. The three women were Clara Decker Young, a wife of Brigham Young; Harriet Page Wheeler Young, a wife of Brigham's brother Lorenzo; and Ellen Sanders Kimball, a wife of Heber C. Kimball, one of the Council of the Twelve. The two children were Isaac Perry Decker, son of Lorenzo's wife by a former marriage, and Zobriski Young, son of the same woman by Lorenzo. Three of the men were listed as "colored"—Oscar Crosby, Green Flake, and Hark Lay. Inventory of property made at this time showed seventy-two wagons of many types—some small, some large and covered—(besides a wagon on which a large leather boat served as wagon box) and a cannon brought along as protection from Indians (who were notoriously afraid of the sound of artillery). Ninety-three horses, fifty-two mules, sixty-six oxen, nineteen cows and assorted dogs, cats, and chickens went along. The expedition was elaborately organized into "hundreds," "fifties," and "tens" (according to the manner Brother Joseph had used in the march to Zion) and was adjured to give strict obedience to the leaders of these units.

President Young chose to travel on the north side of the Platte, though the Oregon Trail, along the south bank, was more distinct and more heavily used. Their road led through Pawnee Indian country.

On Sunday, April 18, the weather was still cold and spring not far advanced. At five o'clock on that day the officers met with President Young who gave them the daily routine. A bugle would sound at five in the morning. Each pioneer would arise and attend prayers before leaving his wagon. Then cooking, eating, feeding teams till seven when the camp would move. Each teamster was to keep beside his team with loaded gun in hand. The order of encampment was to be a circle with the mouth of the wagon to the outside and the horses and cattle tied inside. At eight-thirty the bugle would sound again. At this time all were to have prayers in their wagons and go to bed by nine.

The next day was warm and the pioneers followed the President's orders implicitly. William Clayton, suffering from a toothache, walked beside his wagon and thought of "fixing up a set of wooden cogwheels to the hub of a wagon wheel in such order as to tell the exact number of miles we travel each day." The next day the tooth still ached and Clayton asked Luke Johnson to pull it. "He only got half of the original tooth, the balance being left in the jaw. After this my head and face pained no more than before."

A week went by—a week of hard pulling in soft and sandy loam—day after day of monotonous plodding on a trackless prairie not yet awakened by spring. The brethren nooned on the bank of Loup Fork opposite a Pawnee village and the Indians ran into the water to cross and ask for presents. Young ordered powder, lead, salt, and flour given to them but they continued to beg. Hastily he ordered the wagons to move. At six o'clock they encamped where Looking Glass Creek flows into Loup

Fork. More days on the same pattern and then a day of rest, Sunday the twenty-fifth, with services at four o'clock. "This Earth Was Once a Garden Place," sang the newly formed choir lustily. Then on. The wagons took their own way west across the prairie wasteland. Suddenly April was over. On the last evening of the month the brothers camped beside marshy ground. They were cold and bored and disconsolate. Brother Brigham urged them to dance to warm up and they did so.

On May Day the pioneers caught their first glimpse of buffalo. At once the wagons halted and those brothers appointed buffalo hunters raced their horses toward a herd of over seventy. Wilford Woodruff wrote of the chase, "I then saw that Orrin P. [Porter] Rockwell had three bulls at bay on the prairie. . . . Brother Kimball came up at the same time. We surrounded them and commenced firing upon them. . . ." "The meat is very sweet and as tender as veal," wrote William Clayton. After that the brothers were so often at the kill that President Young forbade them to continue although both sides of the River Platte were black with buffalo for miles, and, as Woodruff wrote, "It looked as though the whole face of the earth was alive and moving like the waves of the sea." There were days when Porter Rockwell or Luke Johnson would capture baby buffaloes and bring them into the camp for the two little boy pioneers to romp with.

On some mornings when the bugle blared the brethren would wake to see flames on the horizon and to feel smoke stinging their eyes. The earth would be black over measureless acres and ashes blown by prairie winds would make their faces as dark as those of their fellow travelers Oscar Crosby, Green Flake, and Hark Lay.

On May 12, the dullness of their day-after-day marching was lessened by William Clayton who, with the aid of mechanic Appleton Harmon, had put into practice the idea he evolved when he had a toothache. He had invented what he called a roadometer and attached it to the axle of the carriage in which he rode. Now its wooden cogs ticked off the miles relentlessly and at the end of every day he could report how much nearer the brethren were to their western paradise.

Spring finally came to the wagon train on the last week of May. On Monday the twenty-fourth, the brethren saw across the river a band of about thirty-five Indians also riding west. After the Mormons had made camp Indians rode across the river toward them, one of those in the lead carrying a United States flag. They were well dressed and impressive people, handsomely adorned. President Young fed them and entertained the chief and his wife overnight. The chief was fascinated by the camp telescope. Through it he looked long at the moon. He may well have been puzzled by a wild dance in which the brethren indulged themselves later.

Now the wagons were rolling into the land of western wonder. For three whole days the high, thin tower of Chimney Rock was constantly in sight and beyond it rose Scotts Bluff like the tumbled walls of a ruined temple. They were almost at the present-day Nebraska/Wyoming line.

Brother Brigham could not forget the dancing in the moonlight on the evening of the twenty-fifth. Life in the camp had become lax in the springtime. The pioneers played cards and checkers and dominoes in their wagons. Some of them played musical instruments and their hearers cavorted to fiddle tunes, dancing with each other and cutting pigeonwings and other figures in the joy of the warming spring season. On the cold, rainy morning of May 29, after the bugle sounded at ten, President Young summoned the camp to gather about the boat-wagon and there spoke his mind. His speech was emphatic and earnest and it ended in burning words of rebuke: "Joking, nonsense, profane language, trifling conversation and loud laughter do not belong to us. Suppose the angels were witnessing the hoe down the other evening, and listening to the haw haws the other evening, would not they be ashamed of it? I am ashamed of it. . . . Now let every man repent of his weakness, of his follies, of his meanness, and every kind of wickedness, and stop your swearing and profane language, for it is in this camp and I know it, and have known it. I have said nothing about it, but I now tell you, if you don't stop it you shall be cured by the Almighty and shall dwindle away and be damned. . . .

"Here are the Elders of Israel, who have the priesthood, who have got to preach the Gospel, who have to gather the nations of the earth, who have to build up the kingdom so that the nations can come to it, they will stop to dance as niggers. I don't mean this as debasing the negroes by any means. They will hoe down all, turn summersets, dance on their knees, and haw, haw, out loud; they will play cards, they will play checkers and dominoes, they will use profane language, they will swear! . . . If we don't repent and quit our wickedness we will have more hindrances than we have had, and worse storms to encounter. I want the brethren to be ready, for meeting tomorrow at the time appointed, instead of rambling off, and hiding in their waggons at play cards, etc. I think it will be good for us to have a fast meeting tomorrow and a prayer meeting to humble ourselves and turn to the Lord and He will forgive us."

The Sunday morning of May 30 was still on the Platte River bottoms but high above the circle of Mormon wagons clouds were scattering in a windy sky. Wakened by the early bugle the travelers could still see Chimney Rock forty miles behind them lifting an admonitory finger. The Black Hills north of the encampment had turned a deep blue, laying grotesque and portentous patterns on the horizon.

At eight o'clock the whole camp gathered near their leader's wagon and raised their voices in Brother William Phelps's hymn:

"The spirit of God like a fire is burning," they sang. "The latter-day glory begins to come forth."

Brother Brigham's rebuke had accomplished its purpose. Wilford Woodruff later wrote of this day: "In the morning I shaved, cleansed my body, put on clean clothing, read a chapter in the Book of Mormon, humbled myself before the Lord . . ."

Soon Woodruff and other chosen leaders followed President Young into a little valley where they "clothed themselves after the manner of the Priesthood." That afternoon they trudged in picturesque procession across the plain for more than two miles to climb a high sandy point. From this they could see to the west a long aisle of bluffs towering on both sides of the river. As they knelt in prayer upon the highest ground they had yet stood upon, Thomas Bullock, who had expected to join them, made note in his journal that he had not been asked to do so. Feeling rejected and sick at heart, he wrote: "I have been deprived of my greatest and most sacred privileges. O my God upon my tears and suffering have mercy on me; wherein I have offended thee, make it manifest to me, that I may repent, whatever it may be."

When the robed priests again entered the circle of their wagons, campfires were spotting the dusk. Somewhere out on the plains a drift of cloud loosed a shower and light from the moon, quick-risen on the eastern rim of the valley, penetrated the falling drops to arch a rainbow above the westward road they would travel on the morrow. Many who had that day promised themselves a holier life saw the gleaming many-colored gateway as a sign of welcome to the country they were seeking.

For all its promise, however, the brethren found the last day of May none the easier. Wagon wheels sank almost to their hubs in sand. Horses and mules strained against the traces. Men bruised their shoulders against the ungiving spokes. Nine miles before nooning—seven and a half more before sunset—and then there was Brother Brigham barking them into a circle beside the straggling cottonwoods and willows of Rawhide Creek.

The morning horn of June first wakened Brigham Young to his forty-sixth birthday. Though his body had thickened and the lines of his face had deepened in the years since Joseph Smith's death, he did not yet resemble in appearance the bearded image which in his later years all of America came to know. He moved with authority and his duties had kept him so much in the saddle through storm and sunshine that none of his companions of the long and wearisome journey resented his leadership.

In the early afternoon came a shout from the lead wagons—"Laramie!" Repeated again and again down the long line, the cry brought a quicker rhythm and the happiness of achievement. By six o'clock the train had covered twelve miles and, rounding a wooded point, trotted into night camp along the River Platte, more than a hundred yards wide. On the low bottoms ash and cottonwood trees lined the water. On the high bluffs beyond, twisted cedars reached into the sky.

"The scene is romantic," wrote Lorenzo Young, sitting in his tent beside the pair of sleeping small boys in his charge. "Opposite stands the ruins of the old fort. On the other side of the river and in front of us is a large black walnut tree." Nearly all the keepers of journals noted that in the center of the camp, tied between two of the highest limbs of a towering ash, hung the tiny dead body of an Indian baby, wrapped snugly in animal skins. The bark of the tree had been peeled off to prevent wild animals from climbing up to eat the high-buried child. Truly they were in the land of the Lamanites with their un-Christian and decadent customs.

On the next day Erastus Snow wrote into his journal: "Today a coal pit is on fire within our circle, and three portable blacksmith shops are in operation; smiths are shoeing horses, repairing wagons, etc."

About ten in the morning Brother Brigham led a delegation across the river to visit the fort. There they found a small gay settlement mostly of French husbands and Indian wives, all under the paternal direction of the agent of the American Fur Company, Mr. Bordeaux. He received them in an upstairs room that Appleton Harmon (who now had begun to look upon himself as the inventor of the roadometer as well as its maker) described as "much like a bar room of an eastern hotel . . . ornamented with several drawings, Portraits, etc., a long desk, a settee and some chairs." There was much bargaining at the company store where the French, knowing well that their customers could buy nowhere else in the area, profited well. Superintendent Bordeaux liked the solemn Mormons who, after the dressing down given them by their leader in the previous week, were well behaved and co-operative, not at all like the wild lot he governed nor the roistering pioneers who had passed the fort in previous months.

Bordeaux told them their passages on the north side of the Platte would be blocked by the Black Hills which slanted steeply down to the water, and urged them to cross the river at once to take the Oregon Trail. The Mormons accepted his advice and for fifteen dollars rented his flatboat for the ferrying of their wagons over the stream.

The crossing began the next morning but was interrupted by a thunderstorm accompanied by hail. Since Bordeaux had told them there had been no rain in the area for two years before their arrival, the travelers regarded this as a further evidence of God's favor. All wagons had crossed before the next noon and at once the expedition set out on the Oregon Trail which was to lead them up the Sweetwater River and across the Great Divide.

Before he left, Brother Clayton, true inventor of the roadometer, consulted the records he had taken with its aid and proudly set up a guideboard on the north side of the Platte: "543-1/4 miles from Winter Quarters," it read, "227-1/2 miles from the junction of the Platte" (north and south branches), "142-1/2 miles from Ash Hollow, 70-1/4 miles from Chimney Rock, 50-1/2 miles from Scott's Bluffs."

The rainy spell continued but the wagon train in the next few days rolled through a narrow ravine, strained up a steep slope, and came out on a rolling prairie gay in the June colors of red, blue, yellow Artemisia (sagebrush of the aster family and known throughout the west by many names—absinthe, wormwood, wild sage, greasewood, mugwort, southernwood). An eagle sailed above the caravan as a light shower from the west caught a moment of sun to set up answering colors in the sky—twin rainbows arching below snow-covered Laramie Peak.

On the rainwashed Sunday morning that followed, the bugle called the brethren to assemble at nine o'clock. While thunder rolled along the horizon they raised their voices in the hymn "With All the Power of Heart and Tongue." Loudly they proclaimed "Angels shall hear the notes I'll raise" and "To God I cried when troubles rose, He heard me and subdued my foes." Wilford Woodruff's journal reads, "The spirit of the Lord was with us."

In the week that followed the Mormons rolled out of the multi-colored prairie into country so wild and grotesque that they were amazed. Between Horse Shoe Creek and the stream called La Bonte they came upon earth so red that William Clayton wrote, "It affected my eyes much from its brightness." Here the travelers saw a toad with a tail and with horns on its head. "It did not jump like a toad but crawled like a mouse." Big black crickets lay so thick on the red soil that it was almost impossible to keep from stepping on them.

Within two weeks after the brethren had left Fort Laramie they had covered a hundred twenty-five miles and reached a second crossing of the Platte. Here with Yankee common sense Brigham Young ordered eight men and a blacksmith left behind to ferry the many Gentile trains behind them across the river at charges sufficient to make a "reasonable" profit.

On they went in a routine that was saved from monotony by the grotesquerie of a landscape growing ever more barren—a horn in the morning and a breakfast made over fires built from sagebrush and dried buffalo dung ("buffalo chips"); then a glimpse of members of the Twelve standing on a high place and sometimes clad in the robes of priesthood, their President kneeling in prayer and the others dropping to their knees beside him, then their faces turned upward to the sky; the cry of the scouts and outriders leading off; the lonely carriage of Brother Brigham leading the train; the squeal of wagon wheels which grease from slain wolves failed to silence; the divisions falling into the procession in the order of accustomed place; the galloping of the teams, when the road was wide enough, to bring the wagons five abreast and lessen the danger of Indian attack.

On June 21, Wilford Woodruff wrote:

I arose early this morning and took breakfast and in company with Brother John we rode clear around Independence Rock. I should judge the distance to be about three quarters of a mile. We examined the many names and lists of names of the trappers, traders, travellers and emigrants which are painted upon these rocks. Nearly all the names were put on with red, black and yellow paint; some had washed out and were defaced. The greatest number were put on within a few years. Some of the names were quite plain of about thirty years' standing. Nearly all the companies that pass by put some of their names on the rock. After going around and examining it we staked our horses and mounted the rock. I went forward and gained the highest point at the south end of the rock which contained the names. After examining it I then went to the north end which is the highest part of the rock. Here is an opening or cavern which could contain thirty or forty persons, and a rock stands on the highest peak of about three tons weight. We got upon this rock and offered up our prayers according to the order of the Priesthood; we prayed earnestly for the blessings of God to rest upon President Young, his brethren, the Twelve, and all of the Pioneer camp and the whole camp of Israel and house of Israel; our wives and children and relatives; the Mormon Battalion, and all the churches abroad, and that the Lord would hasten the time of fulfillment of his promises to Abraham, Isaac, Jacob, Joseph, Lehi, Nephi, Alma, and Moroni, and all the sayings of the Lord concerning the building up of Zion in the last days and avenging the blood of the Prophets and while offering up our prayers the spirit of the Lord descended upon us, and we truly felt to rejoice. . . . I was the first Latter Day Saint that ever went onto that rock or offered up prayers according to the Priesthood.

With their usual business acumen, the Mormons soon station two of their members at the rock to chisel the initials of Gentile travelers into its surface, and charge them for it. Five miles beyond Independence Rock the Mormons stopped again, to see Devil's Gate and hear the roar of the water dashing through perpendicular stone cliffs four hundred feet high. A mile beyond they camped beside the wild current of the Sweetwater. The pioneers could see then, almost obscured by the twilight mists, the distant snowy peaks of the Wind River Mountains and they knew that their long journey would soon be at an end. They had traveled, according to the guide board they erected there, 175-1/4 miles from Fort Laramie.

June 24 began with exasperation for President Young. His team ran away with a wagon but were caught ("by the bit") at the very edge of the river. His best horse (the finest in the expedition) died when herdsman Shepherd Holman nudged him forward with his rifle and the trigger caught in his clothing causing the weapon to fire. Known as the leader's "John" horse, it was the third killed during the trek and caused strong recommendations that the brothers no longer carry loaded guns "with caps upon their tubes." As the day ended Thomas Bullock wrote: "The Sweetwater Mountains are disappearing and the Rocky Mountains are coming into plainer view." Devout Norton Jacob bethought himself of the words of "Old Nephi" as reported in the *Book of Mormon:* "When upon the cross the Savior died for man's sin and wickedness, darkness covered the earth. She trembled and her bosom heaved mightily; . . . here upborn from their lowermost foundations these mighty piles of granite . . .—despite the efforts of summer's suns—have held aloft the ensign of peace."

In that last week of June cold winds from the ice-white slopes of the Rocky Mountains froze milk and water in their pails. Little Isaac Decker and Zobriski Young snowballed each other, their missiles gathered from the ten-foot drifts along the way. Dandelions, strawberries and wild onions bloomed in the sharp dry air of the Sweetwater Valley. On luxuriant grass Wilford Woodruff saw carnelian stones "from the size of a goose egg to a pound"

—more in one hour than he had ever seen "in the rude state or polished and set in breastpins." Red willows stood deep in snow that fringed the river. And on Sunday, June 27, all the Mormons remembered that this day was the third anniversary of the murder of the founder of their faith, Joseph Smith, and of his brother Hyrum. Fittingly on this morning the expedition crossed the Great Divide through the South Pass and all knew that another of the mystic leader's prophecies, that the true Zion would be settled in the Rockies, would soon be fulfilled.

CHAPTER XIV

"Here Is My Home at Last"

As June gentled into July the weather was warmer and the brethren met visitors on the trail—strangers who spoke the dialect of the mountain men and raised it into an intensity that held them spellbound. Brother Brigham and the members of the Twelve felt the historic importance of these meetings with interpreters of the land they were about to enter, and so in turn did the mountain men.

One of these seekers to mold Mormon destiny was old Moses Harris, trader and trapper in the Rocky Mountains for a quarter of a century. "He spoke unfavorable of the Salt Lake country for a settlement," wrote Wilford Woodruff, and William Clayton was depressed by his saying there was "little chance to hope for even a moderate good country anywhere in those regions." The whole countryside was sandy, barren and treeless, the old man said. The Salt Lake Valley was a wasteland of the wild sage.

Heavy of heart the Mormon pioneers pushed on until Brother Brigham at their head heard the jingle of spurs, the hoofbeats of approaching horses. Suddenly out of a hollow appeared three east-bound riders. The leader was forty-two-year-old Jim Bridger, most famous of all mountain men, and he had hardly dismounted before he began to talk, asking that he might be heard not only by their official leader but by the Twelve who served him. By the Little Sandy where they nooned, he told all these about their promised land.

Beside the swift Green River, he said, the mountains stand so close that horsemen cannot pass. On the far side lie level plains that end in hard black rock. It shines in the sun and its edges are so sharp they will cut a horse's feet to pieces. From Bridger's Fort, his home, to Great Salt Lake is about a hundred miles. Along the trail stand sugar trees and cottonwoods. The outlet of Utah Lake runs into Great Salt Lake. It runs muddy and it runs low but its banks are red and white with clover. "There is timber all around the Utah Lake and plenty of blue grass." Great Salt Lake is so big "it takes a man in a canoe three months to go all the way round."

Jim Bridger spoke of mines of gold, of copper and of lead. He knew of lodes of silver and of iron, of sulphur and saltpeter. He said that at the end of Great Salt Lake a bubbling spring spurted hot and cold fresh water, hot and cold salt water, and at the same time manufactured scads of verdigris which the Indians used for green paint with which to daub their bodies. And speaking of Indians, they raise in this area as good corn, wheat and pumpkins as were ever raised in old Kentucky. Wild flax grows in all the valleys. So do grapes and cherries, persimmons and berries. Snow melts on the peaks of the mountains and streams stripe all the slopes, but on the levels are frequent saleratus deserts and lakes surrounded by white salt flats. Nevertheless, said Jim Bridger simply and with a bit of pathos, this country is my paradise and if this people settles in it I want to settle with them. But when some of the brethren said, We will plant corn there, and potatoes, and wheat, Jim laughed and said the winter cold would freeze all such plants.

"I'll give you a thousand dollars for the first bushel of corn you grow in the Great Salt Basin," he said, and Brother Brigham said quietly, "Wait and we will show you."

That night while Bridger was dining with President Young in private, Wilford Woodruff entered into his daily journal his estimate of the famous mountain man and his report: "We found him to have been a great traveler and possessed a great knowledge . . . if what he told us was true."

As he wrote a plague was attacking the camp. "Mountain fever," characterized by headaches, high temperatures, and resultant delirium, had disabled several of the pioneers and in the following weeks it affected many of the men and Clara Decker Young (wife of Brigham), one of the three women, as well. Fortunately its victims recovered in a few days but remained weak and listless for varying lengths of time. Some of the brothers attributed the disease to "mineral saleratus" picked up on the shores of small lakes they passed.

On the last day of June Samuel Brannan who had commanded a group of Mormons who had taken ship "around the Horn" for San Francisco appeared in camp with news of the brethren he had led out and of the Mormon Battalion, many of whom were at Pueblo de Los Angeles. He urged President Young to lead the party to the West Coast and described with lyric fervor the climate and fertility of California. Barley there had no hull on it. There was no necessity to cultivate oats for they grew wild. Clover reached as high as a horse's belly. Wild horses were scattered over the plains. Salmon caught in the San Joaquin River weighed ten or twelve pounds. To all this talk the brethren turned deaf ears. They already mistrusted the shifty Brannan (who was eventually excommunicated) and they were still enchanted by the spell Jim Bridger had cast upon them.

Now that they were in striking distance of their goal the Mormons were in fine fettle and even inclined to regard the hardships they were enduring with humor. On July 3, Thomas Bullock wrote: "We passed a mosquito manufactory, immense swarms of them," and Wilford Woodruff wrote: "The mosquitoes have filled my carriage like a cloud."

Shortly after noon on Sunday, July 4, a detachment of twelve soldiers under the command of Sergeant Thomas Williams crossed the Green River (where the expedition had stopped for the night) and rode into camp in strict formation. Williams said they were in pursuit of horse thieves, as indeed they were, but they were immediately recognized as members of the Mormon Battalion. While they were still in line President Young spoke a few words. Cheer after cheer rose from the brethren. Then according to Thomas Bullock's account the President proposed "Glory to God for their safe return" and all who heard him responded, crying out:

"Hosanna! Hosanna! Hosanna!

"Give Glory to God and the Lamb!"

More soberly wrote Norton Jacobs: "This is Uncle Sam's day of Independence. Well, we are independent of all the powers of the Gentiles; that is enough for us."

The next day was hot, the road was dusty. The pioneers

saw a hard shower descending near the mountains and felt a little wind from it. "In this country," wrote Brother Woodruff, "it rains about the mountains but not much in the valleys and plains." The units of the train stayed farther apart to avoid the dust. They traveled twenty miles to Black's Fork, twenty miles of a trail lined by the blossoms of prickly pears, some red, some yellow, by the bright petals of dog daisies, and found at the end nine wickiups in a beautiful vale, and horses grazing peacefully beside them. Now each day the country grew richer. Cedars flourished in the woods, pines were tall on the mountains, cottonwood roots dug deep into the shallows of the rivers. That night they halted beside a wide-mouthed cave lined with soft sandstone (Redding Cave) and many of the pioneers, boylike, cut their names into its walls. The next day they forded Bear River, nooned at Needle Cliff, and as they made their camp at sunset came a few drops of rain "sufficient [wrote Brother George A. Smith] to cause a full arched rainbow." The brothers were happy.

But in the carriage of Wilford Woodruff there was worry, even fear. President Young had been stricken by mountain fever. His temperature was so high that those who tended him were concerned for his life. Stops became more frequent. On July 13, after consultation among the leaders, it was decided that Orson Pratt should take twenty-three wagons and forty-two of the most able-bodied men as an advance party to explore and make ready the road through the mountains for the rest of the pioneers to follow. Among the list were the names of many men famous in the history of the church and also the three negroes of the lot—Oscar Crosby, Hark Lay, and

Green Flake. Three days later the main camp inched slowly down a steep gulch and were nooning when the long-haired scout, Porter Rockwell, arrived from the advance band to assure them that their party was nearing the canyons that would lead into the Great Basin.

On either side of the lurching wagons that afternoon the red rock walls towered hundreds of feet. "There is a very singular echo in this ravine," wrote William Clayton. "The rattling of wagons resembles carpenters hammering at boards inside the highest rocks. The report of a rifle resembles a sharp crack of thunder and echoes from rock to rock for some time. The lowing of cattle and braying of mules seem to be answered behind the mountains." The playing of band instruments by some of his companions, he added, bounced back from the gulch's walls in exact duplication. To this day the ravine is called Echo Canyon.

On the seventeenth President Young's illness was much worse and the party moved only three miles. From their campsite at Weber River they could see a group of small towers, "Witches Rocks," resembling "old factory or furnace chimneys."

The sun had passed above the amazingly deep defile in which the wagons waited when a band of the camp leaders led by Heber C. Kimball, Willard Richards, and Ezra T. Benson presented themselves in their priestly garments "before the Lord." To Him they offered up their united prayers for their stricken President to be healed, the camp to be prospered, the Saints to be blessed. On their precarious way back "the brethren amused themselves by rolling big rocks down the hill," wrote Thomas Bullock, and William Clayton wrote his own description of the robed Saints rolling "many large rocks from the top of the mountain to witness the velocity of their descent, etc. Some would roll over half a mile and frequently break to pieces."

The bugle sounded at ten in the morning and the brethren met at a cool bowery made in a little grove near the wagon of Willard Richards. Heber C. Kimball then spoke, saying the brethren would do better to pray for the sick and especially President Young, than to scatter off "some hunting, some fishing, and still others climbing mountains." Then he recommended that the whole camp, except President Young and enough men to care for him, set out on the following day to find fertile ground in which to plant potatoes, buckwheat, turnips and other crops. The project was unanimously adopted and on July 20, the major division of the camp was moving in the wake of the advance party, though Heber Kimball, Wilford Woodruff and Ezra Benson stayed with President Young who now was improving rapidly.

Erastus Snow left the main camp in the morning and by strenuous riding overtook Orson Pratt's advance group during the day. He bore messages and on the twenty-first Pratt received a letter from Willard Richards and George A. Smith detailing President Young's advice. The general happiness of the expedition was apparent in a humorous passage dictated by Brother Brigham:

> Prosecute the route as you have hitherto done until you arrive at some point in the Basin where you could hear the potatoes grow, if they had only happened to be there.

On July 22, historic events came with a rush. The main camp rattled down the roughest section of the long road it had covered, but clownish black-and-white magpies tumbled about before them on stumps new-cut for their advance. Sandhill cranes gazed solemnly at them from the banks of steaming hot springs. A hawk sailed above them. The ground "seemed literally alive with very large black crickets crawling around up grass and bushes." Thomas Bullock, camp historian, entered into his journal:

> We succeeded in getting through the narrow part of the canyon about 4 o'clock p.m. when we turned around the hill to the right and came in full view of the Salt Lake in the distance; its islands with their lofty hills towering up in bold relief behind the silvery lake. . . . I could not help shouting hurrah, hurrah, hurrah, here is my home at last.

That night the camp bivouacked beside a little stream almost hidden by tall grasses. Several of the advance party joined them for excited talks. So happy were they all that when hot springs were reported only a few miles away the brethren suggested one would do for a barber shop and that the largest, pouring out of a large rock having a big stone in the middle "would make a first rate Thomsonian steam house."

On the morning of the twenty-third, the pioneers set up a campground on the banks of the stream now called City Creek and exactly at noon Taft turned the first furrow with his plow. The plow broke! It was soon repaired and there were countless other plows.

At two o'clock the brethren began work on building a dam and cutting trenches to carry water into the land. Word came that the oxcart of Lorenzo D. Young, traveling with the President's company, had turned over and little Isaac Decker and Zobriski Young had been pinned inside it. An immediate solution of this difficulty had been obtained by cutting a hole in the wagon cover and dipping for them. Word also came, the best word of all, that Zobriski's Uncle Brigham was much better and would enter the Great Basin on the morrow.

On that morrow President Young, still weak but gaining strength, asked Wilford Woodruff, in whose carriage he was riding, to turn the vehicle so that he might look out over the valley. From his seat, then, the tired commander looked out across the long sea of grass over which a misshapen cedar lifted crooked limbs. Below him, but out of his sight, he knew that those whom he had brought to this Canaan were already enthusiastically at work making the flat acres bordering the wide blue lake a garden spot. "This is the right place," he said to Wilford Woodruff. "Drive on."

"This is the first Sunday that the Latter-day Saints ever spent in the Great Salt Lake Valley," wrote Woodruff on July 25. "We washed, shaved and cleaned up and met in the circle of the encampment. . . . George A. Smith preached an interesting discourse, standing upon the cannon." Other speakers followed and at noon the program was interrupted until the afternoon. At two it began again. At its close President Young, though feeble, spoke. Brother Woodruff entered his memories of the President's speech in his journal later on in the day. The brethren must not work on Sunday, said Brigham Young, and if they did, "they would lose five times as much as they would gain by it, and they must not hunt or fish on that day . . . and there should not one man dwell among us who would not obey these rules; they might go and dwell where they pleased but should not dwell with us."

After a few remarks on the distribution of land, the speaker "warned the Saints against keeping anything that did not belong to them, that if they followed such a course it would leak out and they would stink in the nostrils of Jehovah, the Angels, and the Saints, and though they might live with the Saints and die with them, they would be damned at last and go to hell, for they were thieves and nothing but burning through hell would cleanse them."

Brother Brigham was obviously and audibly himself again.

CHAPTER XV

Celestial Wives

Polygamy was a radical idea in the early years of the nineteenth century in America. Orthodox members of the established churches looked upon it with horror. To many of them it was a practice limited to faraway "heathen" countries where scantily clad and very desirable females lay about in the luxurious seraglios of oriental potentates. The fact that Biblical patriarchs had plural wives, they chose to disregard. But to the lively minds of American experimenters in religious ways of life (and there were many of these), any mode that involved a divagation from previously accepted sexual custom was worthy of consideration. Hence the Shakers—followers of Mother Ann Lee—forbade all sexual intercourse, separated the males from the females in dormitories that allowed of no mixing and waited for the Kingdom of God to arrive in a sinless world. The Oneida Perfectionists, led by John Humphrey Noyes, sought a society in which every member loved every other member with the same amount of affection and passion. "Special love," their name for the romantic pairing known as "falling in love," they regarded as a definite offense against their creed and they punished any couple found guilty of it by banishing one of them to

a distant place, there to await recovery. Sexually therefore, every member of their "Oneida Community" was
mated with every other member who was not of his (or
her) sex.

The leaders of the Mormon Church in its beginnings
soon found that the great majority of Gentiles believed
the Church of Jesus Christ of Latter-day Saints to be a
hoax and a blasphemy. Its claim to having "restored the
only true gospel" (neither Catholic nor Protestant) was
greeted with derision. The narratives within the *Book of
Mormon,* which converts accepted as authentic history,
were denounced by unbelievers as sacrilegious fictions con-
cocted by godless schemers. Since the Mormons themselves
(particularly the followers of Brigham Young) and their
enemies who looked upon polygamous practices with horror, connected the Mormon Church with the "plural
wives" doctrine, confrontations were inevitable.

On the morning of the twelfth of July, 1843, Nauvoo's
newest business structure—a two-story red brick administration building—stood lone in silhouette against the glittering background of the yellow Mississippi. Joseph and
Hyrum Smith climbed the outside stair to the upper office
and found therein twenty-nine-year-old William Clayton
already at work. William was a serious young man, truly
impressed by his recent appointment to the office of the
Prophet's private secretary and bookkeeper. His wide
brow and his deep-set eyes gave him the look of a faithful
confidant who could tell more than his employer had in
secrecy vouchsafed but would not under whatever pres-
sure might be devised.

Joseph had further sealed William's lips by saying to

him: "When I have any revelations to write, you are the one to write them." This announcement had so moved the youthful disciple that he regarded himself (converted to the faith in Lancashire, England, only five years before) as the recipient of God's works only once removed from the divine presence itself.

Joseph and Hyrum were discussing on that fateful summer morning, moreover, the Lord's revelation to His Prophet on a subject that had been given His approval some thirteen years before. Joseph had not informed the brethren of it, however, because of a content shocking not only to non-Mormons but to the members of the little church itself—plural marriage.

Though Joseph had realized then in the second year of Mormon history that the time for writing down and making public had not yet arrived, he and other leaders had (as unobtrusively as possible) taken to themselves additional spouses in the twelve following years. None of these husbands-of-more-than-one had been unaware of the fact that compliance with the revelation would in all probability arouse indignation in his wife. Indeed their acceptance of the divine message had caused such torment and misery among them as to prove more effectively than any other possible test their belief in the Lord and in Joseph Smith as His interpreter. Brigham Young said in 1855 that when Joseph told him of God's will with regard to polygamy it was the first time in his life that he had "desired the grave." Elder John Taylor, who was in time to become third President of the Church, said, "We seemed to put off, as far as we could, what might be termed the evil day."

Said obliging, loyal Hyrum to his brother on that morning at the new brick building: "If you will write the revelation on celestial marriage, I will take and read it to Emma, and I believe I can convince her of its truth and you will hereafter have peace."

Joseph smiled. "You don't know Emma like I do," he said.

"I'm sure I can do it," Hyrum said. "The doctrine is so plain I can convince any reasonable man or woman of its truth, purity, and heavenly origin."

"Well," said his brother hesitantly, "I will write the revelation and we will see."

He sat down, then turned to William Clayton and told him to get paper and be ready to write.

"Get the exact words of the Lord through Urim and Thummim," said Hyrum. "Use those sacred lenses and be sure you're right."

"I don't need to," said Joseph, "I know it word for word from beginning to end."

While Hyrum listened, Joseph began to dictate the revelation and sentence by sentence William Clayton wrote it down. It was long and the Prophet's deep voice was louder than necessary to fill the office.

The sun was nearly at noon height above the water outside when Joseph came to the end.

"Read it through, Brother Clayton," said the Prophet and, in a lighter voice with a Lancashire accent, the secretary began slowly to repeat what he had just written. There was a pause when the revelation ended.

"I could write much more on this subject," said Joseph, "but this will have to do for now."

Hyrum picked up the papers with the momentous writings on them and went out to find Emma. The Prophet and the secretary sat and waited. After an interim longer than the mere reading of the revelation would have taken, they heard Hyrum's step on the outside stair. The door opened and the messenger stalked in and sat down heavily. There was silence.

At last Joseph said, "How did you get on?"

"I've never got such a talking to from a woman in my whole life," said Hyrum hotly. "I didn't know she could get so mad."

Joseph considered this report. Then he said, "I told you you don't know Emma like I do." He took the pages of the revelation from Hyrum and stuffed them into his coat pocket. Then he stood up and walked out into the summer day.

"The Principle," as the Mormons came later to call the belief in plurality of wives, was in the air and led in time to its adoption by the venturesome. A half dozen or more small sects were already favoring multiple female spouses whom they described as "spiritual wives." To this day, however, one may not attribute the teaching of polygamy to Joseph Smith without offending all living members of the Reorganized Church of Jesus Christ of Latter Day Saints. They number about two hundred thousand fervent believers in the *Book of Mormon* and the teachings of Joseph Smith, and they constitute "The Church that did not go West." Aware of the long years in which the Utah church by favoring polygamy had come into disrepute, many of the Reorganized Church members prefer to be dubbed "Josephites" rather than Mormons. This group, which included at its inception Smith's wife, Emma, chose not to join the migration to Utah after Brigham Young had found the way. Among those left behind had been a number of claimants to the murdered Prophet's leadership and authority. Most picturesque of the pretenders was one James Jesse Strang, who eventually led a considerable number of followers to a "Kingdom of St. James" on Beaver Island in Lake Michigan. There, clad in royal robes and wearing a metal crown, he ordered that he be addressed as "King Strang" and, being the husband of five wives himself, offered the benefits of divinely approved polygamy to all his subjects. His reign ended in assassination by two disgruntled "regicides."

The ambitious activities of another aspirant to the leadership, Charles Blancher Thompson, ended ludicrously when his teaching enraged his hearers to the extent that they set upon him violently and he took to his heels. His pursuers gave up the chase only after they had run him for miles across the open prairie.

Lyman Wight took the group who chose him as "Prophet, Seer and Revelator" to Texas. A serious and able man, he immediately pronounced polygamy as a righteous way of life, which ended for this colony only after his death.

By the time of the murder of Joseph and Hyrum Smith, whether the Prophet approved or not, polygamy was being practiced by Mormon leaders, some of them being his best friends. The Principle had not been announced, because of fear that it would cause violent persecutions by the Gentiles, but the number of plural wives was steadily increasing. Somewhat later, ardent believers of Emma Hale Smith's often repeated statement that she was her husband's only mate, sought evidence to bolster their position. "Why," they asked, "did the other women who were said to have married Joseph bear him no issue, though he had fathered many children by Emma?" "Why were these women vague when later questioned about the circumstances of the alleged weddings?" "Why was Joseph so constant in his devotion to Emma?" "Why did his letters show his great dependence on her in time of trouble and why did he not write other of his alleged wives at all?"

These questioners joined to form the Reorganized Church of Jesus Christ of Latter Day Saints at Independence, Missouri. This group has steadily denounced Brigham Young and his associates in the Utah Church as having made the effort falsely to attribute the "Polygamy Revelation" to Joseph Smith. They regarded it as a wicked hoax perpetrated by Young who conspired with others over whom he held authority to give polygamy (through the alleged approval of their martyred prophet) divine authority.

In the years before the lynching of the Prophet Joseph and his older brother, Hyrum, Brigham Young had taken into his household four polygamous wives—the fourth being the sixteen-year-old sister of the first. When he set out as leader of the pioneers on his exploratory journey to Salt Lake, he was the husband of seventeen. Parley P. Pratt, devoted friend of the Prophet and a Western New York State neighbor, took to himself a plural wife in the year before Joseph died. Heber C. Kimball married the first of his more than forty-five wives three years before the death of the Prophet. Mormons were increasingly aware that polygamy, though kept secret, was a growing practice among their leaders before Brigham Young became President of the Church. By 1852, when the Principle was made public, all members of the Utah Church of Jesus Christ of Latter-day Saints had accepted it as the will of God.

The Prophet Joseph regarded the word "Time" as representing the period spent by mortals on earth. In this he followed a precedent set by Jemima Wilkinson—the Publick Universal Friend—whose Keuka Lake colonists were familiar neighbors of the Smith family in the days of Joseph's youth in Palmyra. Death she frequented referred to in her writings as "leaving time."

The Latter-day Saint cosmogony as taught by the prophet-interpreters of God's word (Joseph Smith, Brigham Young, and their successors) revealed that outside the portals of time in the wondrous indescribable land that gave them being before their sojourn on the earth-planet, countless souls awaited the opening of the gateway to another life. Without the experience of living in "Time," this teaching continued, no soul might enter into the eternal happiness of heaven. It was the privilege and the duty of those persons already resident of this world to bring into it, by propagation, as many of the waiting beings as possible in order that they might, through good conduct, prepare themselves for the joys of a never-ending existence beyond the grave. Marriages, if entered into for time and eternity, would continue happily in heaven.

Questions that these teachings inevitably raised were given ready answers. A widow might marry again but for time only and at her death she would be returned to her first husband in heaven. A man, moreover, might marry for eternity not only one woman but many, thus assuring all his wives of a husband in the endlessness of eternity. Wedding for eternity came to be known among the Mormons as "Celestial Marriage" and a man might be "sealed" (Mormon term) to one wife for time only, to another for eternity only, and to a third for both time and eternity. "Celestial wives" could be added to a man's household at such times as he saw fit or as the high officials of the church might advise. Since they would be his mates throughout eternity, it was not deemed sinful for them to enter into the complete marriage state with him when he proposed that they do so. Only couples who were sealed to each other throughout eternity, however, might bear children in the after-death future. Unquestionably sexual intercourse, while still directed only toward the holy cause of producing more Mormons, would be an acceptable activity in the never-ceasing joys of life beyond the silent tomb.

In 1847, while the Mormons were on the move to Utah, the question of religion was certainly not uppermost in their minds.

Hardly had the news of the success of the Pioneer Company reached Winter Quarters back on the Missouri River than the thousands of waiting Mormons were on the road to mountain-circled Zion. Brother Brigham left the valley of the Great Salt Lake in October, but his little party was traveling eastward on a trail already dusty when it came to the Sweetwater River. So great was the exodus from the cabin city that drivers for the rumbling wagons were scarce. Mrs. James Hart of Churchville, New York, with her husband and five of her large family, had been driven out of Nauvoo and had with difficulty arrived at Winter Quarters. There, on July 17, 1847, she wrote to her daughter Mary back in Churchville:

We left Nauvoo on June 2 . . . we arrived at last at Council Bluffs on the Mississippi River which is the most romantic spot you ever saw. It is a hill of hills and while looking at them you can think of nothing but the ocean in a storm with waves rolling mountain high while some have splashed together and turned their course another way. . . .

Later in her long letter Mrs. Hart wrote that her James had joined the Mormon Battalion

. . . to fight for a heartless country that could eventually allow us to be driven from its jurisdiction but we shall soon be where we shall neither protect nor ask protection. . . .

In April, a company of Pioneers consisting of 200 men started to search out a resting place . . . and in June 572 wagons left the camp. . . . Next spring a general effort will be made to move the whole of this church to the same place. . . .

As 500 of our best men were in the army and two hundred Pioneers, it left the camp very destitute of teamsters so when the last company started John and Charles each took charge of a team and they are well on their way to the Rocky Mountains. . . .

Her anxiety for this pair of small boys was tempered with elation, however, for at the junction of the Green and Sweetwater Rivers the party they were serving met that of Brigham Young returning to Council Bluffs. The triumphant leader insisted that further hardships on the long trail would be too much for a pair of youngsters and brought them back to their mother. With justifiable pride, then, Mrs. Hart wrote back to Churchville:

There is not many boys of their age this side of Bear River valley that can tell of the things they can . . . their feet have tramped the soil of the black hills and the Prickly

Pear and their clothes have been washed with the Salratus in its natural state.

The exodus of more than ten thousand Mormons from Winter Quarters required such preparations that the whole encampment rang with the sounds of hammers repairing rusted wheels, of blacksmiths shoeing horses, of families packing their meager possessions. When the first of the companies entered upon the journey across Iowa under the leadership of Dan Spencer, settlers marveled at the long, long parade of covered wagons drawn by mules, oxen and horses. Though the walkers, the riders, the drivers were attempting a journey they had never made before, they were confident. Brother William Clayton, returned from the big valley, had talked of nothing else but the success of the pioneers since his meeting the first west-bound wagon train. He soon tired of repeating the answers to countless questions, however, and he took to Saint Louis his meticulous notes on the twelve-hundred-mile journey led by Brother Brigham. There he persuaded the Missouri Steam Power Press to publish *The Latter Day Saints Emigrants' Guide*, "showing all the Springs, Creeks, Hills, Mountains, Camping Places and all other Notable Places from Council Bluffs to the Valley of the Great Salt Lake." To his title page he added "Remarks on the Nature of the land, Timber, Grass, etc. the whole route having been carefully measured by a roadometer, and the distance from point to point, in English miles, accurately shown." As a result, by the summer of 1848, men who had never been west of Council Bluffs talked learnedly about their forthcoming advance on old Indian villages, Skunk Creek, Sandy Bluffs, Pecanninni Creek, Chimney

Rock, Scotts Bluff, Independence Rock, Devil's Gate, the Black Hills of Wyoming. Doubtless remembering the remark of Harriet Young (Brother Brigham's sister-in-law) on first seeing the Salt Lake Valley—"weak and weary as I am I would rather go a thousand miles farther than remain in such a forlorn place as this"—Clayton added to his foreword a lyric description: "The water is good and very cold. . . . The air is good and pure sweetened by the healthy breezes from the Salt Lake. The grass is rich and plentiful."

Despite this reassurance the winter of 1847–48 was a time of near starvation. Brother Dan Spencer's great command arrived at Salt Lake in September and Brother Brigham, with the mixture of common sense and naïveté which ever characterized him, scattered them in small colonies over the discouraging landscape. Before the turn of the year little towns appeared as if by magic wherever the meandering lines of cottonwood trees or willows gave evidence of wells or flowing water. So in the fall of 1847 began Bountiful, Farmington, Parley's Park, Pleasant Green. The hunters in these little villages barely managed to bring in meat which, added to the supplies of indigenous plants, sufficed to keep the immigrants alive. Had they not been immediately distributed and told to shift for themselves, the thousands of new arrivals might have known famine.

Another danger which President Young foresaw was that, if all members of the church were concentrated in one city, the number of dissatisfied might grow to such an extent that they might constitute danger to the developments he and his colleagues had in mind.

Polygamy, which had brought the Mormons to near

disaster in the preceding decade, would be more easily accepted by the little towns devoting themselves almost exclusively to survival and having less interest in theological argument.

From his high place of authority in Salt Lake City, Brigham went on talking. Sexual intercourse, he said, should be practiced for the single purpose of procreation. Plural wives would consider it their duty to allow the souls waiting at the gates of our world to enter it. And so, with the examples of their President and most of his important associates before them, new settlers began to accept The Principle of which the martyred Prophet had been aware for thirteen years before his death.

The men who desired more wives than one, however, found that they must obtain approval from Mormon leaders. This was possible but generally subject to certain qualifications. Could it be assumed that the prospective husband of a plural wife would be able financially to support more than one family? Did his opinions concur with the teachings of the Mormon Church? Would he give assurances that his first wife would give her consent to his wedding other women and that she would have authority over all others?

Brigham Young took an active personal interest in advising fellow officers of the church on adding new wives to the number they had already married. His recommendation that they do so was usually regarded as a command.

Brigham knew that charges of polygamy had already created a hatred based on shock, jealousy, and fear among the anti-Mormons. Even after he had led his people into "a land nobody wanted" he was not sure that their isolation was a sufficient safeguard against persecution. Therefore he waited until polygamy was an accepted practice among his people before, in 1852, he made public the revelation which Joseph Smith was said to have received from the Lord in the summer of 1831 at Nauvoo.

As more dusty caravans from Winter Quarters toiled up canyon steeps at the end of their long journey, Brother Brigham and his instructed associates directed the ready-made populations toward the awaiting communities. Soon horses, oxen, cows were tethered. The family dogs were barking importantly and the cats curiously inspecting new surroundings. Now the eldest wives assumed their super-intending with relish and the younger scampered about obeying orders. Within the week of arrival the cuttings of Lombardy poplars, brought along from Yankee or York State meadows to diagram new western gardens or to stand against the snow-bearing winds, were set in place and the roots of climbing yellow roses were working into an alien and thirsty sod. When April came after the settlers' first winter and the fiddlers—one provided by Brother Brigham for each village—began tuning for the spring dances, the gardeners added to the nostalgic blooms they had brought from the east (sweep peas and hollyhocks and geraniums) the strong blue blossoms of shooting star, the bold scarlet of monkey flowers, the variegated tints of the sego lily. The settlers delighted in these but their happy satisfaction in them and in their wide acres of wheat and corn soon gave way to panic when their sky was darkened by great blankets of insects—to this day known as "Mormon crickets"—which at once set about destroying all dreams of ample harvests.

Thomas Kane, a young army officer who had vividly

pictured the ruins of deserted Nauvoo, wrote an appalling description of the small but monstrous invaders:

Wingless, dumpy, black, swollen-headed, with bulging eyes in caselike goggles, mounted upon legs of steel wire and clock spring, and with a general appearance that justified the Mormons in comparing him of the spider on the buffalo, the Deseret cricket comes down from the mountains at a certain season of the year, in voracious and desolating myriads. It was just at this season, that the first crops of the new settlers were in the full glory of their youthful green. The assailants could not be repulsed. The Mormons, after their fashion, prayed and fought, and fought and prayed, but to no purpose. The "Black Philistines" mowed their way even with the ground, leaving it as if touched with an acid or burnt by fire.

The less literate Mormons admired this passage but found Brother Brigham's succinct statement, "When you hit one cricket or grasshopper, the air is at once alive with them, and if you kill one, two come to bury him," as more to their taste.

The Mormons had had high hopes for their greening crops. Men, women, children fought desperately against their countless and ravenous foes. When brooms and shovels failed to decrease the despoilers, they carved wooden clubs and flailed the relentless little monsters without ever seeming to diminish their numbers. The sunlight was darkened by them and so were the spirits of the pioneers.

At the moment of their greatest despair they heard approaching a wild and indescribable tumult. The western sky was white with flashing wings. From the blue of the

Great Salt Lake rose a scintillating cloud and from it dropped a rain of gulls. Now the crickets began to disappear into the avid beaks of these birds. Close observers reported that the birds filled their craws with the loathsome creatures, flew back to the lake to drop them, and then sped back for another load.

All day the fluttering multitudes kept up their labors and gradually the cricket onslaught began to lessen. Sunset tinged the shining wings when the invaders had been defeated and the gulls settled upon the lake's blue waters. As they did so, the exhausted human defenders of their crops rushed together to celebrate their victory. From every hill-shadowed valley rose thunderous choruses of gratitude to the God whose emissaries had performed the miracle. Now there would be food throughout the winter and the Mormon farmers lent the full strength of their voices to what had become the Mormon shout of triumph. Raising high their clenched right fists they drove them downward into their cupped left hands to give rhythm and a maximum of emphasis to their words:

Hosannah, Hosannah, Hosannah!
Give glory to God and the lamb!

CHAPTER XVI

The Fading of The Principle

The practice of polygamy, hitherto unemphasized by the officials of the church, had become so obvious to the Mormon settlers in the Great Basin during the early months of colonizing that there could be no doubt of its existence. It was first a privilege of the few high-ranking associates of Brother Brigham. Soon, however, the rank and file, sure that their leaders' acceptance of it as a way of life was favored by divine authority, began to seek plural wives. While the marrying of plural wives either for time or eternity was encouraged by Prophet Brigham, he still feared the effect that the church's adoption of The Principle might have on Gentiles throughout the nation.

Immediately after his public proclamation of it, he knew that he had not underestimated its effect upon non-Mormons of the nation. The Gentile press filled its pages with efforts to express horror and disgust. Denunciations of polygamy resounded from the pulpits of most American churches. Here was a subject on which the respectable and the disrespectable might join in fierce hatred. The prurient-minded enemies of the church exercised their imaginations by claiming that weddings involved Brother Brigham's impregnating the bride before the groom assumed his nuptial privileges and that poetess Eliza Snow demanded similar attention from the new husband. "Stretch a roof over Utah," shouted one rabble rouser, "and you'll have the biggest whore-house in the world."

Meanwhile the church leaders set about trying to convince their followers that the Lord, through his revelations to Joseph Smith, had made it clear that polygamy held divine approval. The saints of the Old Testament, they argued—Abraham, David, Solomon—had taken unto themselves many wives. Why then in modern times should the most devout and dedicated people of the world, those who subscribed most sincerely to the restored Gospel, be forbidden to do so?

The Mormon people had, in their dramatic experience, proved their adaptability beyond question. In the approximate generation-and-a-half in which they lived under polygamy, they again established a successful flexibility. Brother Brigham had made the penalty for men who had committed adultery so severe that many chose the expense of plural households as the lighter burden. But his most successful arguments in favor of polygamy centered about his statement that an unmarried woman who did not marry according to The Principle would, when she died, be facing the bleak prospect of existence through all eternity without a male companion. It became, therefore, the duty of all Mormon men to save the deserving females of the church from so miserable a fate, the desire of all female members to save themselves from desperate loneliness in the life to come. Hence "old maids" became, in public opinion, the most unfortunate of all human beings, and many of them were rescued by pitying Mormon males who wed them with no intent of consummating the marriages.

A number of respected sociologists, among them Kimball Young (a college professor and a grandson of Brigham Young) and Nels Anderson, a trained observer of social groups, have approached Mormon polygamy in the hope of extracting from it such generalities as men of their profession are wont to regard as important. They found, however, that "case histories" depend so much on the individuals involved and that readers are so much interested in the unusual rather than the usual, that they have been led away from their efforts toward generalities into specifics. Adding an extra wife to a married couple cannot fail to produce dramas of the sort that devotees of radio and television (in America at least) have come to know as "soap operas." The number of permutations of such situations did not multiply according to any known formulae and historians have found themselves (whether members of the church or not) led into errors they had not expected to make.

The published "feature stories" (as contemporary news media designate them) found eager readers among Gentile women. The latter wept over the first wife who, on being informed that her husband was bringing a second to their home, climbed through a window and up the roof to the ridge-pole on which she sat under the gleaming pattern of western stars until the pitiless cold of a Utah winter's night stopped the beating of her heart. Another young spouse, when told that her husband had built a nearby house for a prospective second bride, snatched her rifle from its rack and for a week or so sent bullets spaced at regular intervals crashing into the honeymoon cottage.

This action postponed the contemplated wedding indefinitely. A third report (told by a loving wife herself) of the anguish she suffered awaiting the sound of the fall of her husband's second shoe as he entered a newer wife's bed in a neighboring room, wet the pillow of many a Gentile wife with pitying tears.

Juanita Brooks, wholly dependable Mormon historian, has pointed out succinctly that a pioneer Mormon with several wives who worked consistently in his behalf enjoyed material advantages. In her admirable biography of John D. Lee, she tells how two of the younger of John's many wives successfully fought off a would-be jumper of one of their husband's land claims by the strategic use of pans of boiling water. Years later when John D. was being sought by federal officers to answer for many crimes (some of which he had committed), loyal wives scattered across the Utah landscape proved highly valuable by finding him hiding places.

In the sixty-five years during which polygamy received recognition as an approved way of life, the Church of Jesus Christ of Latter-day Saints, ever growing, ever attentive to the words of God as transmitted to them by successive Presidents, Seers, Prophets and Revelators, fitted itself into the pattern that Brother Brigham had outlined for it. Plural wives producing large families were the goal of their society. Friendly to each other, the wives of a single husband taught their children to call their father's other wives "aunt" and to accept their relationships to her and her offspring as natural and productive of affection.

Certain general ideas came into favor. A man's marrying sets of sisters was regarded as advisable because there would be less dissension. Sometimes the man married sisters and their widowed mother, too, to create a well-knit family unit. Sometimes a whole family of father, mothers, and many children would set out from their rambling homestead for Salt Lake City, there to find one more wife who would be acclaimed by all as a desirable addition to their gay cavalcade.

While many young Mormons wished to improve their status in the world-to-come by active obedience to The Principle, they sometimes found themselves curbed by inability to support plural wives. Sometimes they were discouraged by the tastes of maidens who might prefer to marry elderly and kindly "father images," men of higher social status, men of more influence in the church. There were more Mormon *ménages à trois* who lived out the years of polygamy steadily, piously, fruitfully, uneventfully, than such legendary unions as that presided over by Heber C. Kimball, who proved his own dedication to the teachings of the new revelation by wedding more than forty-five brides, thus insuring himself (he believed) of an especially favorable existence in the promised land.

As the structure of the polygamous state grew stronger, its populace steadily became more adaptable. By the mid-fifties many new converts, among them willing prospects for matrimony, were arriving. After the influx of girl immigrants from distant countries, charming foreign accents asserted themselves and a number of pious Mormon males who had felt they could ill afford more wives discovered that they could extend their families to include new spouses for time and possibly for eternity. Dependable Mormon historians have pointed out, however, that although the polygamy revelation had been adopted by the prevailing authorities as the unquestionable doctrine of the entire church, not as large a percentage of the members had acted upon it as non-Mormons have generally been accustomed to believe. The ratio of polygamous families to the Mormon population as a whole, while it varied from time to time, seems never to have risen to more than 15 per cent.

A divorce was an unpopular but always legally possible resort in the polygamy period. A spirited plural wife obtained a decree by declaring she wanted it not on account of her husband's other women, but because she "just couldn't stand the man." Most widely known was the divorce suit of Ann Eliza Webb, Brigham Young's twenty-seventh and last wife, who not only won her legal case but made herself rich by lecturing in the eastern states on the evils of polygamy and the "celestial wife concept." As this fact indicates, Mormonism had become anathema to the Gentiles throughout the country, who were seething with resentment against the growth in the number of polygamous families. As the Congress in Washington became increasingly aware of conditions in Utah, it passed two laws in succession that rendered cohabitation with more than one female illegal.

This action led to a situation that bordered on the ludicrous. Federal officers invaded the homes of the more well-to-do and respected (but polygamous) Mormon citizens to apprehend them. The heads of the families, called "cohabs," were arrested when found, convicted and sentenced to prison. The social status of prison inmates rose to undreamed of heights. Photographers recorded large groups of highly respected Mormon convicts (many of them holding high offices in their church) wearing horizontally striped prison uniforms. These inmates wrote many pathetic letters to their plural wives asking the questions the legally confined have ever wished answered: "How are you?" "How are the children?" "Are our friends who have plural wives able to hide successfully from officers of the law?" "Are our Mormon neighbors providing you and my other wives and children with enough food?" "Will you keep in mind always that the troubles we now suffer are the result of our belief in God's word?" "Do you also believe that the acts of those who would persecute us are sinful?" "Are you serene in the knowledge that the Lord will in His time reward us with His glory?"

Even Brother Brigham, Governor of the State of Utah, spent a night in jail, charged with having more than one wife (the number at the time was over twenty). With his usual self-sufficiency, however, he won acquittal by pleading that the law recognized only the earliest of his living wives as his legal consort.

During the long years when polygamy had settled into an accustomed pattern and young people had been brought up in it with no knowledge of what life in monogamy had been like, misunderstanding between Mormons and their Gentile neighbors grew ever more bitter. Fanatic religious and moralistic groups in the 1860s took upon themselves the mission of saving the nation from "the twin relics of Barbarism," slavery and polygamy. They expected the plural wives of Utah to welcome intervention on their behalf, and were dumfounded when the Mormon ladies coldly informed them that they should mind their own business. When a resident official justice who represented the federal government urged in public that plural wives "become virtuous," Brother Brigham rose in fury to denounce the speaker's insults and to point out to him that the plural wives of Mormonism had never lacked in virtue, and that in the community to which he had come to reside the penalties for adultery were very severe.

By this time the complexion of the Mormon community had undergone changes which had affected the history of polygamy. At the instigation of Brother Brigham and his high-ranking associates the Perpetual Emigrating Fund Company had been formed. Its purpose was to provide enough money to bring to Salt Lake City the converts that had been baptized by Mormon missionaries in foreign countries but could not afford to join their brethren in the American Zion.

The effect of the arrival of hundreds of converts who could not speak English on a population most of whom had been born in New England or upstate New York proved startling. Suddenly Brother Brigham found it necessary to defend the American melting pot he had created. The newcomers had come out of societies of lower economic levels than the Salt Lake Yankees and Yorkers had anticipated, and they differed not only in language but in customs, dress and manners. Blond Swedes found themselves puzzled by the talk of French Mormons chattering ineffectually with dark-visaged converts from distant southern isles. And the explanations of the intricacies of the recently revealed marriage Principle became a matter of deep concern to immigrants, many of whom were hearing them for the first time. They had no sooner become believers in the story of the Farm Boy and the Angel than they were obliged to receive and adopt marriage disciplines that denied all they had learned in the lands from which they had come.

The male converts in these groups found the new limitations difficult; since they were poor, they could not afford to marry until they had won enough land and other material properties to justify their taking on the responsibilities of husbands.

The young women who had come to this far-distant Zion were suddenly aware that materially their own opportunities for matrimony had been enhanced. All men in their communities were possible husbands. A man of middle age, even though he already had several plural wives, might marry a new bride if he could support her. Consideration of these possibilities gave many a marriageable girl motives for musing on her future years.

Almost always, however, the teachings of her new religion were foremost in her mind. As one maiden was reported to have said when given an opportunity of wedding a young Gentile or a polygamous older man prominent among the Saints: "I would rather have his little finger than the whole of a man outside the church."

When in 1877 Brother Brigham was laid away in his self-designed and comfortable walnut casket, polygamy's invincible defender left behind him no champion who could so successfully repel the inroads of Utah's fellow states. Brother Wilford Woodruff, President and Seer, after the troubled administration of President John Taylor, took his problems to the Lord, as every good Mormon still does, and then in 1890 issued a manifesto that in effect prohibited the practice of marrying plural wives. At first a number of Mormons married more wives out of sheer defiance of their President and of a federal law that had been passed by the Congress in Washington some months before. But when they realized that Brother Wilford meant what he said and they were subject to fine and imprisonment, they quickly took to evading government agents as best they could. As in much later days of federal prohibition, these officers traveled in pairs. The most notorious and persistent of the "deps to catch cohabs" were James McGeary and John Armstrong. To them their occupation seemed a sort of game at which they had become very adept. They were a rough pair but not without a kind of grim humor.

The "cohabs" they sought were suddenly disappearing into church steeples, haystacks, cornfields, old cellars, or disguising themselves in women's dresses and sunbonnets. The whole countryside was playing a wild game of hide-and-seek. "Deps" Jack and Jim often dropped in on the families of suspects for occasional meals in the hopes that hunger might have brought the fugitives from their secret lairs, and were usually served with cordial courtesy. When they left to continue their work, they were equally responsive and did not fail to express their hopes that they might find the master of the house in the next time they called.

As the officers continued to increase their populations, the inmates found humor in their confinement and became so used to prison life that they joined those convicted of other crimes in rushing to the upper walls to watch the arrival of new companions and to yell down to them the formerly derisive greeting, "Fresh Fish!"

Pardons, amnesties, completions of sentences were soon to release the Mormon inmates from their incarceration. They and their ancestors had long been accustomed to adapting themselves to unaccustomed conditions. The orthodox Saints found ways of caring for their separate families. The children grew into maturity and accepted their responsibilities, and polygamous marriages were not included among them. The still-misunderstanding federal government constructed a tall building which was meant to receive lonely and heartsick mothers whose polygamous husbands had been forced by the law to live with the wives they had first married, and to its great surprise found no applicants for its use. Large families augmented by the practice of polygamy rode swiftly southward in the darkness of after-sundown skies. Their cattle, their domestic animals, their household properties were massive dust clouds behind them as they raced across an unseen border that slept under the Mexican stars. A man might legally marry as many wives as he pleased and live the life that Brother Brigham and Joseph the Martyr had prescribed for him, always aware of the happiness that awaited him in the glorious finality of life beyond death.

Polygamy would no longer prevail within the limits of the American West nor within the confines of the Church of Jesus Christ of Latter-day Saints. It would rise occasionally among little bands of dissidents who called themselves "fundamentalists" and defied the laws of both church and state. It still does here and there. In Short Creek, Arizona, not long ago, such a group came to the attention of the state's governor and he sent a small army of uniformed state troopers to arrest its members. The polygamists were forewarned and gathered in their high-school yard to wait. Press photographs of them standing there singing "America" with their schoolhouse behind them and their nation's flag blowing above them so softened public opinion that much sympathy was engendered. The separation of wives from polygamous husbands as the trials went relentlessly on seemed tyrannous. The assignment of children to homes in which they had never been and to unknown foster parents seemed an intolerable cruelty.

Polygamy continues to this day in isolated sections of Utah. Now and then a circulation-seeking newspaper or a sensational magazine gives startling headlines to this fact and exaggerates its importance. Few reporters or editors, however, would like to assume the wisdom of a Solomon and distribute children after their mothers and fathers have been sent to prison.

CHAPTER XVII

They Covered Them with Willows

"My grandfather pulled his handcart all the way to Salt Lake," said Willa Rae Reiser, "and every morning he bound his wife's wrists to the tail of the cart. Then when grandma gave out and began dragging, he would stop to let her rest. Otherwise he might find himself going right on without her."

Said Aunt Maggie Nielson down in Bluff on the San Juan River, "In the old days our bishop had a hard time getting around because both his feet had been frozen off when he walked to Salt Lake in the Willie Party of '56."

History among the Mormons is a nearby thing in Utah. It is melodramatic and vivid and the old folk can tell it as they got it from *their* old folk. It still lives in the memories of thousands of families.

When Brother Brigham organized the Perpetual Emigrating Fund Company in 1849, he asked of, pleaded for, ordered his people to add to their tithing sums money for the transportation across the seas to Zion of new Mormons converted by missionaries.

An interesting study might well be made of the reasons why so many foreign converts had enthusiastically accepted Mormon doctrine. Unquestionably, the people of other nations had been moved by the story of the Farm Boy and the Angel. But even devout and orthodox Mormons of today will admit that other motives sometimes obtained in European countries—the lack of jobs in England, the arbitrary pressures that had been brought to bear by other faiths in France and Germany, the wishes of the poverty-stricken in all Europe for a "new start" in a new and free country.

Brother Brigham had soon realized that the church could not afford to finance the kind of emigration it had made possible for foreign converts in the past. Transportation to America by ship was growing more expensive. Rail travel could bring the newcomers only as far as Iowa. Yet thousands who yearned for Zion were waiting to go there. Suddenly an idea that he had rejected before returned with startling force: let them walk! He could get them by water and rail as far as Iowa; let them foot it the rest of the way! With handcarts or wheelbarrows "let them gird up their loins and walk through and nothing shall hinder or stay them."

With his usual dispatch and thoroughness, Brother Brigham began to put his idea into execution. He sent experienced men to Iowa City, which he had chosen as the place where the converts would change from rail trains to carts. Then they could walk the remaining 1300 miles.

On the face of it, the plan seemed ideal—little carts for food and a minimum of clothes——a faith in God and His Prophet for the long walk. Eagerly 534 pilgrims gathered at the Liverpool waterfront to board the charter ship *Enoch Train.* They cheered as her white sails bellied to draw her out of the harbor. Brother Ellsworth, a missionary returning to Zion, would know the way. Behind her would sail the *S. Curling*, filled with more than seven hundred Welch converts and other guiding missionaries going home. It was early spring in England. April would go with them across the water. And at the American wharf in New York, Brother John Taylor would be waiting to lead them to the west-bound train.

They must have made a unique impression as they paraded through New York to the railroad station and piled into cars never meant for cramped, continuous travel. Always to their minds, though, no matter how uncomfortable they were, came visions of the sunny fertile acres of Zion making anticipation bright and happy. Their own brass band of Mormon converts, the "Birmingham Band," was playing then and the feel of solid earth beneath their feet was an invitation to dance—and step out they did—children, old folks and all, whenever the drums and trombones began to speak.

The promise of the beginning of the handcart experiment was not, however, to be completely realized. Not all the little vehicles were awaiting the pilgrims when they tumbled jubilantly from their rail transports. The carts already completed were freshly painted but, unfortunately, built from unweathered hickory or oak hardly worthy of the forthcoming test.

June had arrived in Iowa before the Ellsworth party— 274 of the most eager aspirants for travel—set out on their long walk. Already during their delay they had composed a hearty song with a catchy tune that would carry them marching many a "country mile."

For some must push and some must pull
As we go marching up the hill

As merrily on the way we go
Until we reach the valley O.

At last the command was Forward, and a hundred green handcarts began to roll into and across the river. The "Children of Israel" were on their way to Zion. Scouts were wheeling out ahead of them searching for hostile bands of Gentiles, herds of buffalo that might easily be turned into thundering stampedes, Indians who might cut off the supply wagons at their rear.

The little town of Florence would be a testing goal—three hundred miles away. They reached it in four weeks and stopped to mend the squeaking wheels, adjust the iron rims, make ready to walk the thousand miles left to go.

The sight of so long a procession fascinated the people of the little Iowa hamlets they passed and when darkness was settling on the prairie, their campfires were like reflections of the stars set in the measureless fields of the sky. The sudden outbursts of the brasses from the Birmingham Band brought hurrying crowds from every direction to praise and thank the players and to wonder at the strange method of travel.

At Florence some of their elder guides pointed out to their foreign brothers the crumbling remains of seven hundred houses once built at "Winter Quarters" to protect the refugees driven from Nauvoo. It was from there, the walkers were told, that Brother Brigham and his pioneers had ridden to find another Zion in the Great Salt Lake Valley. They had found it and now a towered city of Mormons was eagerly awaiting the arrival of the first company of handcart immigrants.

With iron rims once more neatly fitted to the wooden

wheels of the carts, the expedition rolled west again toward the distant horizon. Each day the Iowa sun sent down a heat almost unbearable, but the twilight trumpet told the walkers at its end that the distance to Zion was less by about twenty miles. Then on a morning when Brother Brigham had chosen to ride east, he saw a long low cloud of dust clinging to the road ahead and moving toward him. His plan had succeeded! He galloped back to the city and gave orders for the reception of the handcart walkers. When he had finished, the leaders of the procession were walking into Pioneer Square (now Temple Square).

First came a man and his wife and their handcart. On the cart was a legend reading, OUR PRESIDENT, MAY THE UNITY OF THE SAINTS EVER SHOW THE WISDOM OF HIS COUNSEL. The Salt Lake City Band was loudly announcing itself and the Birmingham Band was answering in a wild cacophony, and just behind it three girls were pulling, pushing and worrying their cart along. Hundreds in the crowd that had rushed to line the street were suddenly screaming without knowing they were screaming. Dust was blowing into the square and sunlight was filtering through it. Tears were streaming down the cheeks of men, and women were sobbing.

The celebration of September 26 lasted all day, for hardly had the company of Captain Ellsworth marched through Pioneer Square than Captain McArthur's company was parading the city's streets. Within the next few days a third company, made up entirely of hearty Welshmen, came singing through South Temple Street and immediately settled themselves into the homes of other Welsh Mormon brothers. Then came a long wait and an ominous silence.

Two other companies—those of Captains J. G. Willie
and Edward Martin—had set out from Florence and were
rolling their handcarts somewhere along the trail. They
had reached Iowa City early enough, only to find that
their carts had been made of green wood, the iron rims
of the wheels had come loose and were falling off, and
the provisions they had been promised had not arrived.
Wildly excited by being on the last lap of their long
journey, they had insisted on setting out, regardless of
the fact they had been warned that winter would be
upon them before they would ever reach Zion. They had
hardly begun their journey when they heard the ticking
of little icy snowflakes against the bright-colored leaves
of October. Though they had been delayed by break-
downs, a stampede of a buffalo herd, and by crossing to
the north of the Platte River (at the advice of their long-
experienced brother, F. D. Richards), they decided not to
go back, but to push on. Brother Richards agreed. "Though
it might storm on your right and on your left, the Lord
will keep your way open for you and get you to Zion in
safety."

Apostle Richards added that he would order provisions
which would be waiting for them at Laramie, and so once
more they moved ahead confidently.

Then came the first heavy snowstorm accompanied by
deadly cold. Captain Willie realized the true helplessness
of his situation when he counted his dead: thirteen lifeless, rigid human bodies lay before him. Going back to
Florence was out of the question. And no food was waiting at Laramie. His only recourse was to lessen the amounts
of food and plod on. Strength left the bodies of his fellow
marchers as they received less and less sustenance and

they faltered on the snow-laden path. Even the little children began to stiffen and their mothers told him they could go no farther.

Brother Brigham knew now that the walkers should never have been given permission by his representatives at Iowa City to continue their laboring toward Zion. He had been informed, too, that Captain Martin's company had started later than Captain Willie's. Somewhere on that more than thousand-mile trail between Florence and Salt Lake, two companies of his people, numbering hundreds of men, women, and children, were floundering through the snow, and his agents, who had been ordered to aid them on their way, had failed miserably.

There was a note of desperation in Brother Brigham's voice as he spoke to the assembly at the Autumn Conference Time—the time of warmth and good fellowship in Salt Lake: "My subject is this fifth day of October, 1856, many of our brethren and sisters are on the plains with handcarts and probably are now seven hundred miles from this place: we must send them assistance. The text will be to get them here. This is the salvation I am seeking for, to save our Brethren."

"No oxen," he shouted. "Good horses and mules. Twelve tons of flour and forty good teamsters!"

By the end of that terrible month of the early snows, two hundred fifty teams dotted the white road eastward bound for rescue, but rescue was to come too late for nearly one in four of the walkers. Their plight had been terrible. Never having seen a country like that they were traversing, without a knowledge of the language of its people; chilled to the point where death was an inevitable and welcome release, they struggled on. Zion was not only their one shibboleth, it was their one comforting concept. Surely Zion would be awaiting the pilgrim on his way. Graves had made an ordered aisle leading the way. They covered them with willows. When on the last day of November the last wayfarer of the approximately nine hundred who had begun the journey entered South Temple Street dragging his green cart like a lonely bedraggled child, Brother Brigham abruptly closed the Sunday morning services which had just begun.

"When these persons arrive," he said simply, "I do not want to see them put into houses by themselves. I want to have them distributed in this city among the families that have good comfortable houses. . . . Prayer is good, but when (as on this occasion) baked potatoes and pudding and milk are needed, prayer will not supply their place . . ."

CHAPTER XVIII

"We are ... not going to the moon, nor to any other planet ... but are determined to have a heaven here...."

Brigham Young

Set in a bowl surrounded by snow-capped mountains, Salt Lake City is now one of the most beautiful of American cities, and (from the point of view of a casual visitor) one of the strangest.

Many of the tourists who come to Salt Lake City have preconceived and erroneous concepts of it. A surprising number believe polygamy is still countenanced by the church, though it was banned by that body in 1890 and any member practicing it now would at once be expelled.

Others believe the population of the city is entirely Mormon but Latter-day Saints constitute considerably less than a majority. The most popular joke of the area is the remark, "This is the only city in America where the Irish are Republicans and the Jews are Gentiles." The population of the state of Utah, however, is about 60 per cent Mormon. It would be natural to assume, therefore, that the state is controlled politically by Mormon interests. That the political power of the church is not grossly abused, however, is attested by the fact that Utah has in recent times elected a non-Mormon Governor, J. Bracken Lee. That Mormons often disagree politically is made obvious by Utah's two senators: Wallace Bennet is a Republican; Frank Moss is a Democrat.

"You don't have to be a Mormon to win an election in Utah," said a Salt Lake City politician, "but it helps." It helps also in neighboring Idaho, where over a fifth of the state's population is Mormon. Mormon historians will add that Gentiles who have been elected to public office in these states usually have courted the Mormon vote and listened sympathetically to Mormon suggestions. When Gentile J. Bracken Lee was Governor of Utah he took a firm stand against a bill in aid of education only to yield when elderly David O. McKay, President of the Mormon Church and the most widely respected man (by both Gentiles and Mormons) in the state, proposed a compromise. Mormon public servants during the last half century have made for themselves reputations for honesty and integrity. Few informed Americans will forget the stand of Senator Arthur V. Watkins against the practices of the Joseph McCarthy Committee, or doubt the sincerity of former Secretary of Agriculture Ezra Taft Benson, or deny the high principles of George W. Romney, former Governor of Michigan and recent candidate for the Republican nomination for the Presidency of the United States. Not since Joseph Smith (without hope of election) ran for the Presidency in 1844, has a Mormon sought so prominent an office outside Utah and its environs. Mr. Romney, not then a high-ranking "officer" within the over-all church structure (he was President of the Detroit Stake) had to depend on his reputation as a businessman and the fact that Gentiles look upon Mormons as men of high moral quality to obtain favorable consideration.

This reputation for integrity has been earned, partly

at least, by the fact that, since the Mormons separated themselves from the rest of the national population because of a religious issue, they are more conscious of their history and their creed than are most denominations.

A listening Gentile guest will discover that each member of a Sunday school class will reveal a detailed knowledge of the ugly story of the Haun's Mills' Massacre on October 30, 1838, when sixteen Mormons and two small boys were murdered by a lawless mob. The nonwar that caused President James Buchanan to order a detachment of U. S. Regulars in 1857 to overcome Utah's unruly inhabitants only to receive word that the enemy commander, General Brigham Young, had ended all hostilities on both sides is a favorite history lesson. So are such incidents as the 1879 working of pioneer wagons from Forty Mile Spring down through the Hole-in-Rock to the banks of the San Juan. (Try going back up the Colorado to Hall's Crossing, Hite, and the junction of Dirty Devil River, as this author was once advised by a giggling Sunday school group who knew full well that I knew they were "having me on.")

No other religious group in America "lives" its faith with such emphasis. The Sunday morning men's classes also hear sincere and devout debates on the fine points of their over-all doctrine. Few denominations look upon the existence of heaven with such confidence of its being an assured reality. A recent subject of discussion dealt with a quotation from the work of the French poet St.-John Perse: "And this remains to be said: We live on what is beyond death, and on death itself shall we live." These lines were a favorite quotation of the late Dag Hammarskjöld. They happen to be a distillation of one of the major teachings of the *Book of Mormon* and its Prophet, Joseph Smith.

Earnestness in church endeavors is regarded as an essential to social acceptance among the Saints. Indeed, the life of the average Mormon is more likely to be concerned with church committee meetings than with casual parties. A visitor who familiarizes himself with the daily life of Utah Mormons will soon discover that the structure of church life is so comprehensive that it keeps most members as busy as they can be and still make a living. This does not mean that they do not indulge in social amenities. The hospitable Mormon housewives are justly proud of their cooking and few committee members return to their homes after a meeting without feeling a little too full of cake (Mormon women are especially skilled at making cakes) and fruit drinks—lemonade, orange juice, grape juice.

Though the *Deseret News*, church-owned daily paper, is widely subscribed to by both Gentiles and Mormons, the church members are inclined to the constant reading of the *Church News* whose moralistic editorials strenuously attack matters which the eastern press is inclined to ignore. Indeed it attacks what its editor regards as immoral dress with the same frank, earthy invective that Brother Brigham Young, speaking on the same subject, was accustomed to use from his pulpit nearly a hundred years ago. Said a recent issue:

> Only disgust is expressed by the average man who sees otherwise respectable women exposing themselves when sitting down. There certainly is nothing decent about this exposure. And where is the comeliness? Does any woman

suppose that she looks her best when revealing such intimate areas as are openly put before the public gaze on almost every side?

In men it is called indecent exposure, and they are put in jail. With women similar exposure is called fashion.

Quite far removed from the attitude of the *Church News* today is a recently published magazine called *Dialogue*. It welcomes the contributions of non-believers as well as young Mormon intellectuals who happily discuss the seeming inconsistencies of such church doctrines as free agency (which insists on man's liberty of choice) and unquestioning obedience to the church (which seems to deny it). The Managing Editor, Eugene England, has expressed this journal's attitude with complete clarity in an admirable sentence which reads: "A man need not relinquish his faith to be intellectually respectable, nor his intellect to be faithful."

The scholar who delves deeper than the tourist into contemporary Mormon living will soon feel that he has miraculously entered a period similar in its moral and spiritual overtones to that of America as a whole in the nineteenth century when the churches satisfied more than their declared function with such events as church suppers, Wednesday-night prayer meetings, Sunday-School picnics, and evangelistic revivals. When to these are added such patriotic solemnities as Pioneer Day, Fourth of July celebrations, and an attitude of praise and admiration toward men in public service, it is not surprising that the historian comes away from Utah with the conclusion that the primary virtues which made the nation what it is are here more honored than in most regions of America.

Hence Mr. Romney's taking a day off for fasting and prayer for divine guidance before making his decision to seek the governorship of Michigan, though it may have seemed unusual to eastern politicians, even a vote-getting gesture to some cynics, aroused no especial comment among his fellow Mormons. When it is remembered that founder Joseph Smith recorded his asking the Lord for advice on the most homely, day by day decisions during the early days of the church he founded, Mr. Romney's act proved to be completely in the Latter-day Saints tradition.

The curious visitor in Utah will feel at first that there is little difference between what the Mormons believe and the widely accepted creeds of other denominations. He will discover that the very name of the denomination, the "Church of Jesus Christ of Latter-day Saints," assumes acceptance of the Christian Bible and a desire to abide by its teachings. It will be obvious to him that, like other American church members, the Mormons admire the Christian virtues. It will be only after more serious research that he will find that the Mormons hold many beliefs that are dissimilar to those generally accepted by the most popular denominations of the nation. Among these the most significant and comprehensive is that the Lord desired a restoration of the only true gospel which in the centuries since its inception has been misinterpreted by Christian churches. The Lord described the true gospel to Joseph Smith in detail and it is now the gospel of the Mormon Church.

A second difference from other creeds lies in the Mormon's conviction that Joseph Smith was chosen of God to bear witness of sacred truth and was therefore a "latter-day saint" and as true a prophet as any named in the Bible.

Thirdly, the Mormon belief is that the *Book of Mormon* was given through Joseph to the world and is as divinely inspired as the Bible. Brigham many years later answered the question which is often asked by puzzled Gentiles, "What became of the golden plates after Joseph had translated them?" Brigham, in a sermon delivered in Utah, said: "When Joseph got the plates, the angel instructed him to carry them back to the Hill Cumorah, which he did. Oliver [Cowdery] says that when Joseph and he went there, the hill opened, and they walked into a cave, in which there was a large and spacious room. He says he did not think, at the time, whether they had the light of the sun or artificial light; but it was just as light as day. They laid the plates on a table; it was a large table that stood in the room. Under this table there was a pile of plates as much as two feet high, and there were altogether in this room more plates than probably many wagon loads; they were piled up in the corners and along the walls. The first time they went there the sword of Laban hung upon the wall, but when they went again it had been taken down and laid upon the table across the gold plates; it was unsheathed, and on it was written these words: 'This sword will never be sheathed again until the kingdoms of this world become the kingdom of our God and his Christ.'"

While many denominations have had their say about the evils of smoking tobacco and of excessive drinking, it is the Mormon belief that Joseph Smith received a divine revelation in which he was told that smoking and the drinking of alcoholic liquors are against the will of God.

This revelation known as the *Word of Wisdom,* is accepted by all orthodox Mormons who faithfully abstain from the practices described. In its original wording it reads in part:

> That inasmuch as any man drinketh wine or strong drink among you, behold it is not good, neither meet in the sight of your Father. . . .
>
> And, again, strong drinks are not for the belly, but for the washing of your bodies.
>
> And, again, tobacco is not for the body, neither for the belly, and is not good for man, but is an herb for bruises and all sick cattle, to be used with judgment and skill.
>
> And again, hot drinks are not for the body or belly.

Hot drinks were interpreted to be coffee and tea. The Mormon makes no effort, however, to convert his Gentile acquaintances to his diet. A frequent and kindly Mormon remark is, "I do not drink alcoholic liquors but please order whatever you wish."

Another Mormon custom that is now apparently dying out has been the wearing of underclothes known as "Temple Garments" or "Sacred Garments." These garments usually made of knitted cotton were early introduced into Temple rituals and all Mormons of both sexes were, until recently, expected to wear them. They are similar in design to an old-fashioned "union suit." Over both breasts, the navel, and the right knee are significant symbols. The garments once covered the body from the neck to below the shin, but they have been modified by shortening to above the knee. Long custom and the fact that they are considered protective against both physical harm and evil influence have resulted in the most orthodox wearers' keeping at least a part of them continuously touching the body. Even if he is taking a bath and about to put on clean underwear, he will not release the worn garment until some part of the fresh one is on him. A Mormon student at a college dance once told an interested Gentile that he could tell a "good Mormon girl" by the fact that he could see, just under the top of her off-the-shoulder dress a roll which was evidence of her having pushed her sacred garment down an inch or so. During World War I Mormon recruits found Gentile officers sometimes unsympathetic toward the wearing of non-GI underwear. In World War II, the Korean War, and the war in Vietnam, however, the church made special allowances.

Joseph Smith in his own account of his answer to a question, "Will everybody be damned but Mormons?" answered, "Yes, and a great portion of them unless they repent and work righteousness."

This reply led to questioning with regard to the fate of ancestors who had lived and died before the founding of the Mormon Church and to a comforting answer. The Lord revealed to Joseph that baptizing of the dead by proxy would result in their being able to associate with their friends and relatives in the world to come. At once Mormons began looking into the histories of their own families. They launched a well planned program in genealogical research which has become the largest undertaking of its kind in the world. Church records, medical records, cemetery records, legal records have been scanned a state at a time and in some cases the results are nearly complete. Mormon genealogists have worked assiduously in most of the United States, Scandinavia, Germany, France, England,

and many other countries. Mormon or Gentile, the geneal-
ogist is welcomed to card files now available in Salt Lake
City. The number of cards approximates more than thirty
million and still grows rapidly. The number of proxies
who have been willing to be baptized for the dead has of
necessity grown too. The proxies are frequently young
people who are happy to lend themselves to the ceremony
that will bring the countless dead into the Mormon heaven.
(The ritual requires total immersion.)

A Gentile sociologist once asked, "What do Mormons
do at five o'clock in the afternoon in place of our tea
parties and cocktail parties?" The Mormon considered this,
then said, "I guess that's when the children come home."

The children's home-coming is a considerable event in
the Mormon day. A large number of progeny is a status
symbol. The *Deseret News* delights in publishing photographs of grandparents surrounded by a dozen sons and
daughters and what seems to be an astronomic number of
grandchildren. The church itself, although not officially
opposed to birth control, encourages large families. It
teaches that countless spirits await life in this world into
which they must be born as children. It urges that they
be given the opportunity for the experience which is
looked upon as a preparation for an eternally happy life
beyond the grave.

While many rich members of other faiths have attributed
their financial successes to the blessings of God, the Mormons are the only group that is convinced that the Almighty gives them prosperity because they are Mormons.
As early as March 29, 1834, Prophet Joseph and Oliver

Cowdery, as representatives of the Mormon faith, agreed to enter into the following covenant with the Lord:

> That if the Lord will prosper us in our business and open the way before us that we may obtain means to pay our debts, that we be not troubled nor brought into disrepute before the world, nor His people; after that, of all he shall give unto us we will give a tenth to be bestowed upon the poor in His church, or as He shall command; and that we will be faithful over that which He has entrusted to our care, that we may obtain much; and that our children after us shall remember to observe this sacred and holy covenant; . . .

It would appear that the terms of this offered compact have been so meticulously observed by both parties to it during the last hundred and thirty-six years that Mormons have the strong conviction that the Lord will grant to an earnest L.D.S. (Latter-day Saint) material rewards for loyalty to his church. The Gentile newcomer to Salt Lake City will be somewhat surprised to find that the Mormon Church itself is one of the biggest Utah corporations. One of its most impressive properties is the resplendent white Hotel Utah. Another is the Deseret Book Store which does a thriving business in general trade books as well as in the sale of volumes concerning Mormons and Mormonism. A third is the city's largest department store, usually referred to as "ZCMI" (Zion's Co-operative Mercantile Institute), which, until recently, sold the approved "sacred garments." Other of the investments of the Church include mines, railroads, real estate, in many of the states of the nation and in many European countries as well. The Church authorities are not inclined to make public any estimates of its wealth, but aside from all profits from its investments, the returns from the payment of tithes from its growing membership amount to several millions of dollars a month. When Bracken Lee, Gentile politician, once announced that the Church has an income of a million a day he was generally believed though he later withdrew the statement. A better concept of the Church's money resources is the fact that in 1969 it was considering the sale of much of its Florida ranch lands for a hundred million dollars. This was said to be the largest land transaction ever contemplated between two private entities in the United States. It has led many a Mormon of today to call to the brothers' attention that when Brother Brigham was opposing the intentions of some of his flock to join the 1849 rush to California he spoke out flatly: "The true use of gold is for paving streets, covering houses, and making gospel and making culinary dishes; and when the saints shall have preached the gospel, raised grain and built up cities enough the Lord will open up a way for a supply of gold to the perfect satisfaction of His people."

The riches of the Mormon Church have enabled it to adopt a steadily expanding missionary program. Its thousands of volunteer missionaries, chosen from its most likable and intelligent young men, labor in pairs for periods of two years each throughout the world, receiving their expenses from their pious parents or friends. While their success in obtaining new converts in the United States is not startling, in Latin American countries and in the southern islands of the Pacific, such as Fiji, Samoa, and Tonga, it is remarkable. Great Britain, from the beginnings of the Church, has been a fertile field. Last year its membership rose to over 71,000. Mormon authorities have announced that it will be erecting a church building a week for the next twelvemonth. In France there were a thousand conversions last year and more than twice that many are expected next year. The number of memberships in West Germany has doubled within the past year.

The administration of the Church's funds has given Gentiles credence in the oft-repeated remark, "No Mormons go on Federal relief." It is true that the Church "takes care of its own" and that a deserving Mormon in a period of hard times has only to ask his bishop (equivalent of an unsalaried pastor in a Protestant church) for food and clothing and he will be given an order on the "Bishop's Storehouse" that will satisfy his needs. The recipient must be willing to contribute work on a Church project, however, in return for aid. An administrator of the Church Welfare Department once said, "Just as there are lazy Presbyterians there are sometimes lazy Mormons— who find going on federal relief preferable to going to work." The Bishops' Storehouses, by the way, are very comprehensive and every effort is made to keep the recipient of their supplies from feeling that he is accepting charity. Foods which were at first placed in unlabeled cans are now packaged in containers marked THE DESERET CANNING COMPANY, in order that those who obtain them will not feel unfavorable reactions of even a psychological nature.

The Mormon Church holds two Conferences annually —one in the spring and one in the fall. These are attended by Mormons from all over the world. They sit on the hard seats of the great Tabernacle, listen to the thunderous organ, the great chorus of the choir, and exhortations from Mormon leaders. A member who has served on the New Zealand Mission proves it by speaking for five

minutes in the Maori language. A Hawaiian speaker will
report on the beauty of the Hawaiian Temple and on the
encouraging flow of Hawaiian converts. Young missionaries report on the remarkable increase of conversions
in France. A Swedish representative will tell how things
are in Scandinavia, always a strong outpost. Sometimes
a bearded old-timer may scold the audience of more than
ten thousand, urging Mormon young people not to associate with Gentile youths. He may speak of basketball
games he has attended where Gentile smoking has befouled
the air and Gentile drinking of spirits has created disorder. He may warn his hearers against disobedience of
the mandates of the Church. Under the Mormon principle
of free agency, he may say, you have the right to make
your personal choice, but flouters of the Church are likely
not to go far in Mormon circles thereafter, and he adds,
"Remember to pay your tithes and don't nurse your nick-
els." After the services successful businessmen, college presidents, inventors, ranchers, political leaders will be pointed
out by proud fellow-Mormons. During a Conference
the dining room of the Hotel Utah seems to have a
yellow glow. It is caused by the thousands of orange
drinks which are the Mormons' favorite substitutes for
forbidden coffee and tea. The waitresses in the hotels
are weary to the point of desperation. "I'm LDS myself,"
says one of them, "but I don't like people of any kind
in great groups." To an elderly elevator operator a Gentile
says, "What a tremendous gathering," and the reply is,
"Think that all this came about through God's word to a
teen-age boy."

The Mormons are earnest believers in recreation as a
part of their educational program. Their stake houses (a

[205]

"stake" is a unit made up of wards and the wards are the smallest group of the church structure) frequently contain, besides small classrooms for discussions by male members of the Church, an auditorium for Sunday School, in which wives and children participate with their husbands and fathers, a large hall which may be used both for basketball games and dancing.

Next summer on the first moonless night of August many thousands of Mormons and Gentiles will gather at the foot of a little New York State hill near Palmyra to await the beginning of the annual pageant of the Church of Jesus Christ of Latter-day Saints—a dramatic telling of the story of Mormonism by the people who know it best—the Mormons. The audience knows that soon, with the aid of poetic words, appropriate music, sonorous and significant action, the strange story will unfold. Above them, indirectly lighted against the open sky, will stand the statue of Moroni, wrought by a Danish sculptor. From all over the world the minds of the young missionaries will be turning to Cumorah. So will the thoughts of the people of Salt Lake City and of Utah's desert towns guarded by Lombardy poplars and gay with New England's yellow climbing roses. At Cumorah Hill thousands of Mormons will be singing "Come, Come Ye Saints." As the last words of the hymn die out a sudden stream of light will flood the stage below Moroni's human counterpart. The angel will speak, and in the silence that follows his words, the poor farm boy will answer.

CHAPTER XIX

From the Author's Notebook

PIONEER VOCABULARY OBTAINED FROM MORMONS AND THEIR CONTEMPORARIES

Belching: Tattling, babbling, "squealing."

Beot: A "boast speech." Making a boast speech was a common custom among Anglo-Saxon warriors in the days before 1066.

Besom (bezum): Broom.

Blackleg: Swindler.

Bogus-makers: Counterfeiters.

Bogus: Counterfeit money.

Breakfast: "A good cup of coffee and a fowl with some corn bread or dodger."

Butter print: Butter mold or stamp.

Davy: Affidavit.

Dodger: Corn bread.

Doughhead: Bonehead; a stupid person.

Good crater: Apparently an alcoholic drink.

Grannyism: An old-womanish expression.

Greasewood: A stunted, prickly shrub found on alkaline plains in western U.S. When dry, it burns with great heat.

Grecian bend: A posture fashionable among women in which the body is bent sharply forward from the hips.

Henry: A popular kind of rifle, forerunner of the Winchester rifle.

Hum, to feel out of: To feel out of sorts.

I can't come it: I can't believe it; or, I can't accomplish what I am trying to do.

In tongues: The pure language which Adam and Eve spoke in the Garden of Eden.

A "Joe Miller": Referring to a book of jokes by Joe Miller.

Juke, to: To dodge.

Kinnikinic: Indian pipe smoke.

Massasauga: Prairie rattlesnake.

Mericats: Indian name for American non-believers in Mormon faith.

Mormon brake: Wagon brake on wheel.

Mormon buckskin: Bailing wire.

Mormon cricket: Grasshopper.

Mormon rice: Hulled corn.

Mormon weed: American jute, variously known as Indian mallow or "velvet leaf."

Mormonee: Indian name for believers in Mormon faith.

Piñon bread: Bread made with piñon nuts.

Plain mountain English: Talk without affectation.

Rabbit-brush: A non-inflammable weed.

Rim-rocker: Compulsive wanderer of mountains.

Rocky Mountain herring: Grayling.

Saline slope, to take the: To take to one's heels; decamp.

Slippery elm poultice: A poultice made from the inner bark of the slippery elm tree.

Snowshoe-mouth deep: To the top of one's snowshoes.

Soggum candy: Sorghum candy.

Sour bread: Sour-dough bread.

Spanish soap root: Root used by Mexicans for washing; top like pineapple, makes suds like soap.

Squawbush: A rank-smelling, sprawling shrub (sumac) found from Illinois and Texas to the Pacific coast.

Stink-finger brush: A malodorous weed from which pioneers wove water jugs.

Stout of corn: A standing sheaf of corn.

Tottlish canoe: An unsteady canoe.

Valley tan: First referred to tanned hides of cattle burned by Mormons; later, a kind of whiskey.

Wimble: Lively, brisk; weavings of willow branches.

FOLK EXPRESSIONS AND IDIOMS

"Straight as a loon's leg."

"A caution to Crockett."

"Go to hell crosslots."

"We would 'a' skinn'd 'em as quick as Crockett would a coon, and then eat 'em alive without leaving a grease spot."

"Steeped and boiled by hot drinks and tanned by tobacco juice."

"His breath smells as if he had swallowed a stillhouse."

Food the first winter in Salt Lake City: "Sego roots and thistles boiled up with buffalo robes."

Spring 1848: "Goggle-eyed crickets with clock-spring legs."

"Scrimped-up dandies": Dudes.

A "pulling weeds" religion.

"We're a-hunting a wheelbarrow's nest."

"Leeks and onions"—superfluous and unimportant details.

"As fit for travel as a powder magazine in Hell."

"Make catfish bait of him": To kill.

"Some men will chase a picayune five thousand miles when I would not turn around for it."

"Oh, granny, granny, what a long tail our puss has got."—A satiric remark to a braggart.

Influenza, politically called "the Tyler gripe" or grippe.

MORMON HUMOR:

Heber Kimball was rebuked for swearing at oxen. He replied, "It's the only language they understand."

Kimball is reported to have said:

"Sure I'll pray for our enemies! I'll pray they may all go to Hell."

"They can't cut me off. I repent too damn fast!"

"How many of you in this congregation would give your lives for the church?" The raising of hands was unanimous. Then said Brother Golden Kimball: "How many of you would give fifty cents to the Church?"

"If the Lord won't keep his damn fool promises, then I will."

"But if this war is ever over, I'll be damned if I ever love another country!"

He said he loved his fellow men but he loved some of them better than others.

"I have often told you that all my lazy hairs were gone."

"Damn such fixings, they are not of God."

Other samples of Mormon humor are:

"A Mr. Thompson of Kansas Territory has built a prairie ship, or wagon, to be propelled by wind, in which he proposes, with thirty companions, to make a voyage to the Rocky Mountains next June. We hope Mr. Thompson will choose some able-bodied men, and take plenty of grub along." (*The Mormon*, March 17, 1855)

"They were sure they could send that boy to Hell or Texas, they did not care which."

"When Jehovah fights, they would rather be absent."

"They have not got as much force as would draw a mosquito off its nest."

"Brother David Fullmer this morning talked about working all our lives upon a wall if it were necessary; but the wall we contemplate making here is not a breakfast spell (not to be done in a short time).

Description of a pious New Englander: ". . . a strict, religious, holy, down-country, eastern Yankee, who would whip a beer barrel for working on Sunday."

"From the time of his birth he never knew mirth. He was candid and sober and never would play, and minded his father and mother in toiling all day."

A Swedish farmer went into the little town near which he lived to get a loan from the bank to pay for his seed for the coming year. First he went to the cashier and the cashier said, "It's been a bad year. You'd better see the vice-president" and the vice-president said, "It's really been a bad year, and you'll have to see the president." So he went to the president and the president just said, "No, we are not giving out loans this year."

So he went outside and he saw his nearest neighbor who said, "Did you get your loan from the bank?" And he said, "No I didn't. They made me see the cashier and the vice-president and the president and you know, if you was to take them three fellers and stuff them in a barrel and roll it downhill, there'd be a son-of-a-bitch on top all the way down."

George A. Smith explained the coming of the Saints

to Utah: "We came here willingly because we were obliged to."

Heber C. Kimball, being always honest in the principle of tithing, decided to turn his nice-looking black horse in, and said to his son Golden: "I want you to take that horse over to Bishop Hunter and turn it in before my soul crumples up!"

When Brother Golden Kimball was preaching a funeral sermon, he looked up at the congregation and saw the very man whose praises he had been reciting listening eagerly. "Who in hell's dead here anyway?" demanded Brother Golden.

Three men entered a bookshop in Salt Lake City. "Brother," said one of them, "we have come for some books." "But," said the salesman, "we do not sell books on Sunday." "We are a long way from home. Can't you possibly take care of us?" "Sorry," said the salesman, "but we have an ironclad rule. It would not be right to do business on Sunday. How big is your order?"

I want devils to gratify themselves; and if howling, yelling, and yelping will do you any good, do it till you are all damned

. . . and you can then go on your way to hell without a grunt.

He will deliver him to the fowls of heaven, and his bones shall be cast to the blasts of the wind, for he lifted his arm against the Almighty, therefore the Lord shall destroy him.

The devil, . . . personified in some of the religionists, begun to prick up his ears and jump and kick and run about like Jim Crow, calling for rotten eggs to help in the wake.

Hyrum Smith compared lawyers to polliwogs, wigglers and toads: ". . . were made in gizzard-making time, when it was cheaper to get gizzards than souls . . . if a soul cost $5, a gizzard would cost nothing. Like tree toads, they change color to suit the object they are upon."

Brother Brigham names and denounces "fornication pants":

"My pants button up here where they belong that my secrets that God has given me should not be exposed. I favor pants that open on the side; they are plenty good enough and speedy enough."

"Many preachers say that fiddling and music come from Hell, but I say there is no fiddling, there is no music in Hell." (*Brigham Young*)

ANGELS AND HOW TO IDENTIFY THEM

How was this known to be a bad angel? By the sandy color of his hair . . . and by his contradicting a former revelation.

If a person is sick they would like to be visited, comforted or healed by an angel or spirit. . . . A man shipwrecked would like to be instructed in the way of escape . . . from a watery grave. In case of extreme hunger, a loaf of bread brought by an angel would not be unacceptable. If murderers were lying in wait for a man on a certain road, an angel would be useful to tell him to take another road.

All the difference between men and angels, men are passing through the day of trial that angels have already passed through. They belong to the same family that we do but they have proven themselves worthy only of an exaltation of a state of angels.

Names of some of the builders who worked on the Kirtland Temple:

Gad Yale
Starry Fisk
Salmon Gee
Peter Shirts
Sebe Ives
Jacob Bump
Erastus Rudd

MEDICINE: REMEDIES AND DISEASES

Brother Ezra Thayre's cure for colic in horses: A three-penny paper of tobacco, half an ounce of copperas and two tablespoonfuls of cayenne pepper, and a bottle filled with water when he could not procure whiskey. One half of a bottle constituted a dose, and would almost invariably cure a sick horse in a few minutes, and is worthy of re-membrance. Brother Thayre called his medicine "18 by 24."

". . . would . . . lie down on the ground when their

blood was heated, and they would be liable to take diseases, such as fever and ague, which are prevalent in this climate."

"The Mississippi water is more healthful to drink than the spring water, but you had better dig wells from fifteen to thirty feet deep, and then the water will be wholesome. . . . All those persons who have not been accustomed to living on a river or lake, or large pond of water . . . get away . . . back to the hill where you can get good well water. If you feel any inconvenience, take some mild physic two or three times, and follow that up with some good bitters. If you cannot get anything else, take a little salts and cayenne. If you cannot get salts, take ipecacuanha, or gnaw down a butternut tree, or use boneset, or horehound."

"Calomel doctors will give you calomel to cure a sliver in the big toe . . . and calomel on an empty stomach will kill the patient. Lobelia doctors will do the same."

February 8, 1876: "Several prisoners down with Epi Zooda."

Cure for cholera: Drench the victim in cold water and feed him whiskey thickened with flour to the consistency of starch.

Cure-all: Three drops of turpentine and a tablespoon of castor oil.

Favorite tonic: White sage tea.

Fever and cold: Hale's Honey of Horehound and tar.

Hall's Sicellian Hair Remover.

Indigestion: Hastetters Bitters.

Inflamation of the bowels: Pulverized charcoal and sweet milk boiled together.

Favorite emetic of Indians: Leaves of the white willow.

Lumbago and venereal complaint: A bottle of Magic Oil.

Measles: Spirits and cayenne pepper.

McClains Pills.

PROVERBS AND APHORISMS

A man too afraid of doing wrong seldom does right.

Every dog will have his day and a bitch two afternoons.

If you wish to know how to have your bread fall butter side up, butter it on both sides.

A man is a bad teamster who runs his team on the worst road.

It is no use living among hogs without a snout.

As the old birds crow, the young ones learn.

It's a pity to throw tea away after it has spoiled half a gallon of the best American creek water.

Perfect solitude cannot exist where owls do not hoot at night.

When we shake our own bushes, we want to catch our own fruit.

Every tub has to stand upon its own bottom.

If you kill a cricket, two come to bury him.

Any man who will make whiskey to sell would sell the Kingdom of God for a picayune.

If this is not in the Bible it is somewhere else, and if it be true it is just as good as if it were in the Bible.

A man should have three wives: two to beg and one to sew sacks.

Holidays

No sooner had the Mormons selected the little town in which they would live, and harvested their first good crop, than they were filled with gratitude to the Lord for their successes. Happy over the profits of their endeavors, and gay with prospect of more to come, they indulged their love of social gathering with holidays—each named for the crop in which they had labored. They loved—and still love—the opportunity of taking days off to celebrate the joys brought to them by their fertile fields. Like their Indian neighbors, they always sought to express their gratitude to whatever the elements, their seeds, their weather, their animals had brought them. And so they rollicked in honor of the happy events that circled their lives. Each of their merry, idle days was given a special name and on it they gave thanks for the blessings they had received. They crowded into their little towns to exult in a thanksgiving for their ripened peaches, their fattened turkeys, their reddened strawberries. They danced on their level fields remembering their cherries, their chickens, and their pigs. They watched their calendars to make sure that they did not miss Hereford Day or Sheep-Shearing Day. They also celebrated the Fourth of July, Pioneer Day and all the patriotic days observed by the nation as a whole.

Bibliography

BOOKS—NONFICTION

Abbey, Edward. *Desert Solitaire*. New York: McGraw-Hill Book Company, 1968.

Anderson, Nels. *Desert Saints*. Chicago: University of Chicago Press, 1942.

Arrington, Leonard J. *Great Basin Kingdom*. Cambridge, Massachusetts: Harvard University Press, 1958.

Arrington, Leonard J., and Hansen, Garby B. *"The Richest Hole on Earth."* Logan, Utah: Monograph Series, Utah State University Press, 1963.

Ashton, Wendell J. *Theirs Is the Kingdom*. Salt Lake City, Utah: Bookcraft Co., 1945.

Bach, Marcus. *Faith and My Friends*. New York: The Bobbs-Merrill Co., Inc., 1951.

Bailey, Paul. *The Armies of God*. Garden City, New York: Doubleday & Company, Inc., 1968.

Beadle, J. H. *Life in Utah; or the Mysteries and Crimes of Mormonism*. Philadelphia: National Publishing Company, 1870.

Beals, Carleton. *Our Yankee Heritage*. New York: David McKay Co., Inc., 1955.

Bennett, Archibald F. *Searching with Success*. Salt Lake City, Utah: Deseret Book Company, 1962.

Bennett, Wallace F. *Why I Am a Mormon*. New York: Thomas Nelson & Sons, 1958.

Beston, Henry. *American Memory*. New York: Farrar & Rinehart Inc., 1937.

Billeter, Julius C. *The Temple of Promise, Jackson County, Missouri*. Independence, Jackson County, Missouri: Press of Zion's Printing and Publishing Company, 1946.

Billington, Ray Allen. *America's Frontier Heritage*. New York: Holt, Rinehart & Winston, 1966.

Billington, Ray Allen. *The Westward Movement in the United States.* Princeton, New Jersey: D. Van Nostrand Co., Inc., 1959.

Birge, Julius C. *The Awakening of the Desert.* Boston: Richard G. Badger, The Gorham Press, 1912.

Birrell, Verla. *The Book of Mormon Guide Book.* Salt Lake City, Utah: Verla Birrell, 1948.

Blassingame, Wyatt, and Glendinning, Richard. *Men Who Opened the West.* New York: G. P. Putnam's Sons, 1966.

Brodie, Fawn M. *No Man Knows My History.* New York: Alfred A. Knopf, 1945.

Brooks, Juanita. *John Doyle Lee.* Glendale, California: The Arthur H. Clark Company, 1962.

Burton, Richard F. *The City of the Saints.* New York: Alfred A. Knopf Inc., 1963.

Calverton, V. F. *Where Angels Dared to Tread.* New York: The Bobbs-Merrill Company, 1941.

Cannon, George Q. *The Life of Joseph Smith, the Prophet.* Salt Lake City, Utah: The Deseret News, 1907.

Clark, Elmer T. *The Small Sects in America.* Nashville Tennessee: Cokesbury Press, 1937.

Clayton, W. *The Latter-day Saints' Emigrants Guide.* Saint Louis: Republican Steam Power Press—Chambers and Knapp, 1848.

Cleland, Robert Glass, and Brooks, Juanita. *A Mormon Chronicle: The Diaries of John D. Lee—1848–1876.* Two volumes. San Marino, California: The Huntington Library, 1955.

Commager, Henry Steele, and Nevins, Allan. *The Heritage of America.* Boston: Little, Brown and Company, 1939.

Corbett, Pearson H. *Jacob Hamblin, the Peacemaker.* Salt Lake City, Utah: Deseret Book Company, 1952.

Cowley, Matthias F. *Wilford Woodruff.* Salt Lake City, Utah: The Deseret News, 1916.

Creer, Leland Hargrave. *Utah and the Nation.* Seattle, Washington: University of Washington Press, 1929.

Davis, Inez Smith. *The Story of the Church.* Independence, Missouri: Herald Publishing House, 1943.

Day, Robert B. *They Made Mormon History.* Salt Lake City, Utah: Deseret Book Company, 1968.

Dellenbaugh, Frederick S. *A Canyon Voyage.* New Haven and London: Yale University Press, 1908 and 1926.

De Voto, Bernard. *The Year of Decision 1846.* Boston: Little, Brown and Company, 1942.

Doctrine and Covenants—Pearl of Great Price. Salt Lake City, Utah: Church of Jesus Christ of Latter-day Saints, 1949.

Edwards, F. Henry. *A Commentary on the Doctrine and Covenants.* Independence, Missouri: Herald Publishing House, 1958.

Evans, John Henry. *Joseph Smith, an American Prophet*. New York: The Macmillan Company, 1933.

Evans, John Henry. *Our Church and People*. Salt Lake City, Utah: Deseret Book Company, 1924.

Evans, Richard L. *May Peace Be With You*. New York: Harper & Brothers, 1946.

Federal Writers' Project. *Kansas*. New York: The Viking Press, 1939.

Federal Writers' Project. *Nebraska*. New York: The Viking Press, 1939.

Federal Writers' Project. *The Oregon Trail*. New York: Hastings House, 1939.

Flanders, Robert Bruce. *Nauvoo—Kingdom on the Mississippi*. Urbana, Illinois: University of Illinois, 1965.

Frost, James Arthur. *Life on the Upper Susquehanna, 1783–1860*. Columbia University, New York: King's Crown Press, 1951.

Furniss, Norman F. *The Mormon Conflict, 1850–1859*. New Haven: Yale University Press, 1960.

Glazier, Captain Willard. *Peculiarities of American Cities*. Philadelphia: Hubbard Brothers Publishers, 1883.

Grant, Heber J. *A Short History of the Church of Jesus Christ of Latter-day Saints*. Published by the Church of Jesus Christ of Latter-day Saints, 1938.

Green, Nelson Winch. *Fifteen Years Among the Mormons*. New York: H. Dayton, 1859.

Greene, Laurence. *Headlines of the Past*. Garden City, New York: Garden City Publishing Co., Inc., 1936.

Griffin, Clifford S. *Their Brothers' Keepers*. New Brunswick, New Jersey: Rutgers University Press, 1960.

Gunther, John. *Inside U.S.A.* New York: Harper and Brothers, 1946.

Hafen, LeRoy R., and Rister, Carl Coke. *Western America*. New York: Prentice-Hall, Inc., 1941 and 1950.

Hamburger, Philip. *An American Notebook*. New York: Alfred A. Knopf, Inc., 1965.

Hanks, Sidney Alvarus, and Hands, Ephraim K. *Scouting for the Mormons on the Great Frontier*. Salt Lake City, Utah, Deseret News Press, 1948.

Hansen, Klaus J. *Quest for Empire*. East Lansing, Michigan: Michigan State University Press, 1967.

Harris, T. George. *Romney's Way—A Man and an Idea*. Englewood Cliffs, New Jersey: Prentice-Hall, Inc., 1967.

Hawgood, John A. *America's Western Frontiers*. New York: Alfred A. Knopf, Inc., 1967.

Hinckley, Gordon B. *What of the Mormons?* Salt Lake City, Utah: Church of Jesus Christ of Latter-day Saints, 1947.

Hinds, William Alfred. *American Communities*. Chicago: Charles H. Kerr & Company, 1902.

The History of the Reorganized Church of Jesus Christ of Latter Day Saints. Volume 2. Independence, Missouri: Herald House, 1952.

Holbrook, Stewart H. *The Yankee Exodus.* New York: The Macmillan Company, 1950.

Hunter, Milton R. *Beneath Ben Lomond's Peak.* Salt Lake City, Utah: Deseret News Press, 1944.

Hunter, Milton R. *Brigham Young, the Colonizer.* Independence, Missouri: Zion's Printing and Publishing Company, 1945.

Hymns. Church of Jesus Christ of Latter-day Saints. Salt Lake City, Utah: Deseret News Press, 1948.

Jenson, Andrew. *Encyclopedic History of the Church of Jesus Christ of Latter-day Saints.* Salt Lake City, Utah: Deseret News Publishing Company, 1941.

Jonas, Frank H. *Western Politics.* Salt Lake City: University of Utah Press, 1961.

Journal of Discourses by President Brigham Young and Other Church Leaders. Volumes 1–26, 1854–86.

Kane, Mrs. Thomas. *Twelve Mormon Homes.* Philadelphia: William Wood, 1874.

Kennedy, J. H. *Early Days of Mormonism.* New York: Charles Scribner's Sons, 1888.

Kipling, Rudyard. *From Sea to Sea—American Notes* and *City of Dreadful Night.* Volume 9. Garden City, New York: Doubleday, Page and Company, 1899 and 1907.

Kirkham, E. Kay. *Research in American Genealogy.* Salt Lake City, Utah: Deseret Book Company, 1956.

Kjelgaard, Jim. *The Coming of the Mormons.* New York: Random House, 1953.

Knowles, J. Harris. *A Flight in Spring.* New York: J. Harris Knowles, 1898.

Larson, Gustive O. *Prelude to the Kingdom.* Francestown, New Hampshire: Marshall Jones Company, 1947.

Lee, John Doyle. *The Mormon Menace.* New York: Home Protection Publishing Co., 1905.

Linn, William Alexander. *The Story of the Mormons.* New York: The Macmillan Company, 1923.

Loud, Grover C. *Evangelized America.* New York: The Dial Press, 1928.

Lundwall, N. B. *The Fate of the Persecutors of the Prophet Joseph Smith.* Salt Lake City, Utah: N. B. Lundwall, 1952.

McGavin, E. Cecil. *Mormonism and Masonry.* Salt Lake City, Utah: Bookcraft Co., 1947.

McGavin, E. Cecil. *Nauvoo the Beautiful.* Salt Lake City, Utah: Stevens & Wallis, Inc., 1946.

McMaster, John Bach. *A History of the People of the United States.* Eight volumes. New York: D. Appleton-Century Company, Inc., 1938.

Martin, Stuart. *The Mystery of Mormonism.* London: Odhams Press Limited, 1920.

Miller, David E. *Hole-in-the-Rock.* Salt Lake City, Utah: University of Utah Press, 1959.

Missouri Writers' Project. *Missouri.* New York: Duell, Sloan & Pearce, 1941.

Morison, Samuel Eliot, and Commager, Henry Steele. *The Growth of the American Republic.* New York: Oxford University Press, 1942.

Mulder, William, and Mortensen, A. Russell. *Among the Mormons.* New York: Alfred A. Knopf, Inc., 1958.

Mullen, Robert. *The Latter-day Saints: The Mormons Yesterday and Today.* Garden City, New York: Doubleday & Company, Inc., 1966.

Nibley, Hugh. *The Myth Makers.* Salt Lake City, Utah: Bookcraft Co., 1961.

Nibley, Preston. *Brigham Young, the Man and His Work.* Independence, Missouri: Zion's Printing & Publishing Company, 1936.

Nibley, Preston. *Exodus to Greatness.* Salt Lake City, Utah: Deseret News Press, 1947.

Nibley, Preston. *Joseph Smith, the Prophet.* Salt Lake City, Utah: Deseret News Press, 1944.

O'Dea, Thomas F. *The Mormons.* Chicago: University of Chicago Press, 1957.

Parry, Edwin F. *Stories About Joseph Smith, the Prophet.* Salt Lake City, Utah: Deseret News Press, 1951.

Peterson, Emma Marr. *The Story of Our Church.* Salt Lake City, Utah: Bookcraft Pub. Co., 1952.

Piercy, Fredrick Hawkins. *Route from Liverpool to Great Salt Lake Valley.* Cambridge, Massachusetts: The Belknap Press of Harvard University Press, 1962.

Pratt, Parley Parker. *Autobiography of Parley Parker Pratt.* Salt Lake City, Utah: Deseret Book Co., 1950.

Provo—Pioneer Mormon City. (Compiled by the Workers of the Writers' Program of the Work Projects Administration for the State of Utah.) Portland, Oregon: Binfords & Mort, 1942.

Pyper, George D. *Stories of Latter-Day Saint Hymns.* Salt Lake City, Utah: Deseret News Press, 1939.

Reiser, A. Hamer. *History of the Church for Children.* Salt Lake City, Utah: Deseret Sunday School Union Board, 1945.

Ricks, Joel. *Helps to the Study of the Book of Mormon.* Published by the Church, 1916.

Roberts, B. H. *A Comprehensive History of the Church of Jesus Christ of Latter-day Saints, Century 1.* Six volumes. Salt Lake City, Utah: Church Deseret News Press, 1930.

Robertson, Frank C. *A Ram in the Thicket.* New York: Hastings House, Publishers, 1950.

Schindler, Harold. *Orrin Porter Rockwell—Man of God/Son of Thunder.* Salt Lake City, Utah: University of Utah Press, 1966.

Scott, Reva. *Samual Brannan and the Golden Fleece.* New York: The Macmillan Company, 1944.

Sjodahl, J. M. *An Introduction to the Sudy of the Book of Mormon.* Salt Lake City, Utah: Deseret News Press, 1927.

Smith, Joseph Jr. *Book of Mormon: An Account Written by the Hand of Mormon, Upon Plates Taken from the Plates of Nephi.* Palmyra, New York: E. B. Grandin, 1830.

Smith, Joseph Jr. *Book of Mormon: An Account Written by the Hand of Mormon upon Plates taken from the Plates of Nephi.* Translated by Joseph Smith, Jr. Salt Lake City, Utah: Published by the Church of Jesus Christ of Latter-day Saints, 1950.

Smith, Joseph. *History of the Church.* Seven volumes. Vols. I–VI by J. Smith. Vol. VII from the manuscript history of Brigham Young and other original documents. Introduction and notes by B. H. Roberts. Salt Lake City, Utah: The Deseret News, 1932.

Smith, Joseph Fielding. *Essentials in Church History.* Salt Lake City, Utah: Deseret News Press, 1950.

Smith, Joseph Fielding. *Teachings of the Prophet Joseph Smith.* Salt Lake City: Deseret News Press, 1938.

Smith, Joseph Fielding. *The Way to Perfection.* Independence, Missouri: Genealogical Society of Utah, 1949.

Spencer, Clarissa Young, and Harmer, Mable. *Brigham Young at Home.* Salt Lake City, Utah: Deseret News Press, 1947.

Sperry, Sidney B. *Problems of the Book of Mormon.* Salt Lake City, Utah: Bookcraft Co., 1964.

Stafford, Helen Cortez. *Sweet Love Remembered.* Salt Lake City, Utah: Deseret Book Company, 1946.

State and Local Government in Utah. Salt Lake City, Utah: Prepared and published by Utah Foundation. 1954.

Stegner, Wallace. *The Gathering of Zion.* New York: McGraw-Hill Book Company, 1964.

Stegner, Wallace. *Mormon Country.* New York: Duell, Sloan & Pearce, 1942.

Stenhouse, Mrs. T. B. H. *"Tell It All."* Hartford, Connecticut: A. D. Worthington and Company, 1874.

Stewart, Georgia Metcalf. *How the Church Grew.* Independence, Missouri: Herald Publishing House, 1959.

Stewart, John J. *Mormonism and the Negro*. Orem, Utah: Community Press Publishing Company, 1960.

Stout, Hosea. *Autobiography of Hosea Stout*. Reprinted from the *Utah Historical Quarterly*. Volume XXX, 1962.

Talmage, James E. *The House of the Lord*. Salt Lake City, Utah: Deseret Book Company, 1968.

Talmage, James E. *The Story of "Mormonism" and the Philosophy of "Mormonism."* Salt Lake City: The Deseret News, 1914.

Tanner, Annie Clark. *A Mormon Mother*. Salt Lake City, Utah: Deseret News Press, 1941.

Tanner, J. M. *James Jensen*. Salt Lake City, Utah: The Deseret News, 1911.

Taylor, Samuel Woolley. *Family Kingdom*. New York: McGraw-Hill Book Company, 1951.

Times and Seasons. Volume 1. Salt Lake City, Utah: Modern Microfilm Company,

Turner, Wallace. *The Mormon Establishment*. Boston: Houghton Mifflin Company, 1966.

Tuttle, Charles R., and Durrie, Daniel S. *The State of Iowa*. Chicago: Richard S. Peale and Company, 1876.

Tyler, Alice Felt. *Freedom's Ferment*. New York: Harper & Brothers, 1944.

Wallace, Irving. *The Twenty-Seventh Wife*. New York: New American Library, 1961.

Werner, M. R. *Brigham Young*. New York: Harcourt, Brace, and Company, 1925.

West, Ray B. Jr. *Kingdom of the Saints*. New York: The Viking Press, 1957.

Whalen, William J. *The Latter-day Saints in the Modern World*. New York: The John Day Company, 1964.

Whipple, Maurine. *This Is the Place: Utah*. New York: Alfred A. Knopf, 1945.

Whitney, Orson F. *Life of Heber C. Kimball, an Apostle; the Father and Founder of the British Mission*. Salt Lake City, Utah: Published by the Kimball family, 1888.

Widtsoe, John A. *Discourses of Brigham Young*. Salt Lake City, Utah: Deseret Book Company, 1925.

Widtsoe, John A. *How the Desert Was Tamed*. Salt Lake City, Utah: Deseret Book Company, 1947.

Widtsoe, John A. *In a Sunlit Land*. Salt Lake City, Utah: Milton R. Hunter and G. Homer Durham, 1952.

Widtsoe, John A., and Harris, Franklin S. Jr. *Seven Claims of the Book of Mormon*. Independence, Missouri: Press of Zion's Printing and Publishing Company. (no date)

Winther, Oscar Osburn. *The Great Northwest*. New York: Alfred A. Knopf, 1947 and 1950.
Young, Kimball. *Isn't One Wife Enough?* New York: Henry Holt and Company, 1954.

BOOKS—HISTORICAL FICTION

Bean, Amelia. *The Fancher Train*. Garden City, New York: Doubleday & Company, Inc., 1958.
Fife, Austin and Alta. *Saints of Sage and Saddle*. Bloomington, Indiana: Indiana University Press, 1956.
Fisher, Vardis. *Children of God*. New York: The Vanguard Press, Inc., 1939.
Furnas, J. C. *The Devil's Rainbow*. New York: Harper & Brothers, 1962.
Lyman, Albert R. *Voice of the Intangible*. Salt Lake City, Utah: Deseret News Press, 1936.
Snell, George Dixon. *Root, Hog, and Die*. Caldwell, Idaho: The Caxton Printers, Ltd., 1936.
Sorensen, Virginia. *The House Next Door*. New York: Charles Scribner's Sons, 1954.
Sorensen, Virginia. *A Little Lower than the Angels*. New York: Alfred A. Knopf, 1942.

PERIODICALS

Brigham Young University Studies. Volume IX, Number 3, Spring 1969. Volume VIII, Number 3, Spring 1968.
Dialogue: A Journal of Mormon Thought. Volume 1, Number 1, Spring 1966, and all issues to date.
Kimball, Stanley B. "The First Immigrants to Nauvoo." *The Improvement Era*. March 1963.
Missouri Historical Review. Volume LXII, Number 2, January 1968.
Mulder, William. "The Mormons in American History." *Bulletin of the University of Utah*. Volume 48, Number 11, January 14, 1957.
New York History. Volume XXII, Number 2, April 1941.
Reader's Digest. Volume 90, Number 538, February 1967.
Reznick, Samuel. "A Traveling School of Science on the Erie Canal in 1826." *New York History*. Volume XL, Number 3, July 1959.

Utah Historical Quarterly. Volume XXIV, Number 4, October 1956. Volume XXVII, Number 3, July 1959. Volume XXIX, Number 1, January 1961. Volume 35, Number 4, Fall 1967.

Utah Humanities Review. Volume I, Number 1, January 1947. Volume II, Number 1, January 1948.

PAMPHLETS

Barney, Gwen Marler. *The Mormons and Their Temples*. Salt Lake City, Utah: Bookcraft Co., 1959.

Bennett, Archibald F. *Proving Your Pedigree*. Salt Lake City, Utah: Deseret Sunday School Union Board, 1951.

Carter, Kate B. *Pioneer Humor*. Salt Lake City: Daughters of the Utah Pioneers, May 1952.

Everton, Walter M. *The Handy Book for Genealogists*. Logan, Utah: Walter M. Everton, 1949.

The Exploration of the American West Before 1880. National Archives Publication No. 64-6. National Archives and Record Service. General Services Administration. Washington, 1963. Gardner, John W. "Uncritical Lovers, Unloving Critics." Commencement Address at Cornell University. Ithaca, New York. June 1, 1968.

Highway Adventures. Third Edition. Utah Oil Refining Company. 1950.

Kirkham, E. Kay. *The ABC's of American Genealogical Research*. Salt Lake City, Utah: E. Kay Kirkham, 1954.

Lee, Hector. *"The Three Nephites."* University of New Mexico Publications. Albuquerque, New Mexico: University of New Mexico Press, 1949.

Pratt, Elder Orson. *The Laws of Stewardship and Consecration*. Copied verbatim from *The Deseret Semi-Weekly News*, Volume 9, Number 50, July 21, 1874.

Ralston, Russell F. *Succession in Presidency and Authority*. Independence, Missouri: Herald Publishing House, 1958.

Smith, Elbert A. *Differences that Persist*. Independence, Missouri: Herald Publishing House, 1943.

Smith, Elbert A. *Faith of our Fathers Living Still*. Independence, Missouri: Herald Publishing House. (no date)

Thomas, H. W. *"An Evaluation of Mormonism in 1882."* Chicago: *Chicago Tribune*, 1882.

Woodruff, Wilford. *The Necessity of Having the Holy Ghost*. Copied verbatim from *The Deseret Weekly News*. Volume 53, Number 21, November 7, 1896.

THESIS

Ellsworth, Richard Grant. "A Study of the Literary Qualities in the Diary of Hosea Stout." An English Thesis (M.A.) Brigham Young University, 1952.

TAPE

"This is the Place." British Broadcasting Corporation. Provided by Church Information Service, Church of Jesus Christ of Latter-day Saints, Salt Lake City, Utah. (60 minutes)
The Sally Goheen Tape Office of the Geneseo Historian, Geneseo, New York.

INDEX

L7